Finding PHIL:
Four Traits for Conquering Chaos

Michael Frickstad

MOCH *Arts*

Published by MOCH Arts
Parker, Colorado 80134

To all the manifestations of PHIL in my life: friends, mentors, students, family, Diane, and God Himself.

Meet PHIL

LET ME INTRODUCE YOU to PHIL.

PHIL is a friend I turn to when life is overwhelming. When everyday headlines and talking heads scream, "Chaos reigns!—COVID19 pandemic, violence, disaster, corruption, destruction, hatred. Escape futile!" Times when even unwrapping a candy bar is a daylong task.

Times of frustration and worry.

Times like now.

Oh, I try to put on a brave face, claiming "Meh. Chaos doesn't scare me. I taught high school English," but like everybody else, I quiver before the innumerable, unimaginable forces bent on destroying our world. On the positive side, though, decades of teaching, the trials of life, and PHIL's counsel have taught me a very important truth: Like the ravages of puberty, chaos can be conquered. When things are starkly, mind-bendingly nuts, there are ways through the mayhem, ways to help you confront, tolerate, and eventually overwhelm the forces trying to annihilate you.

Are they easy ways?

Sometimes. Sometimes, not so much. Often they require years of living, learning, and midnight revelations. Oh, not a blinding light, a burning bush, or a bugling elk. More often a nagging reflection on a day's events, like the voice of a guardian angel guiding you through the crisis if you would only listen. A voice like PHIL's.

I'm not saying PHIL is a guardian angel, some celestial creature complete with wings and a halo, flying around in a flowing white robe, performing miracles. Although at times that would be nice. No, I would have noticed that presence long ago, but to tell the truth, I only recently learned to recognize the influence PHIL has had in my life. Let me tell you the story.

For years, I have viewed Sunday morning church service —rightly or wrongly—as a refuge from the commotion of existence. Usually, it has worked. A special song will speak to me, or I'll hear profundities in the pastor's sermon. Like a faithful student, I use my trusty ballpoint pen and the bulletin to take notes, scrawling scripture references and insights wherever there's room with the sincere intent to decipher and mull over them hours later. Usually, my wife Diane sits quietly next to me.

One particular Sunday, however, as the pastor walked to the front to begin his sermon, before I could even take the cap off my pen, Diane snatched it and my bulletin, leaving me lost and befuddled. Now what was I supposed to do?

Without even whispering an explanation, she began writing. Curiously, I leaned over to see what she had written, but I couldn't read it. Abruptly, she handed back my pen and bulletin, patted my hand, then returned her attention to the sermon.

At the top of the bulletin, I found "DC—Informal Prayer Walk—invite people to pray at the same time."

What the heck? The writing was clear; that wasn't the problem. However, the words confused me.

After service, I opened my mouth to speak, but Diane, who has a habit of starting my sentences for me, usually with something important we're supposed to do, interrupted me.

"I had an idea and I had to write it down before I forgot," she explained. "So we're going to Washington in a few weeks, right?"

I love going with her to DC. It's a perfect getaway for me. She works and I explore. What did she have in mind? I was confused. Warily, I answered, "Ri-i-ight?"

"Well, what if on one of the days after work, we visited the seats of power and prayed, not for individuals or specific conduct, but for God to guide the people who work there?"

"That sounds—"

She interrupted again. "And what if while we were walking, others back here in Colorado or our friends in Michigan and Minnesota joined in, walking and praying where they are? A virtual prayer walk for a God-sized movement."

I recognized the sparkle in her eyes. This wasn't just a discussion between husband and wife. When she had had ideas like this before, they were not just hers. This was a message. Rather than question her, I was to open myself to the possibilities.

"Okay," I nodded.

Even though I knew that was the right answer to make, all the way home I wondered, "How is this going to work?"

It didn't matter. We were going to do it.

All day and into the night back at the house, I deliberated, rationalized, and evaluated to the point I could not sleep, pondering what we would pray for, how we would publicize the event, and how it would be successful. In the dark of our bedroom, the last two answers came easily. As if I had thought of them myself.

Publicity? *Facebook and word of mouth.*

Prospects for success? *Not your problem. Just do it and God will take care of the effects.*

The subject matter of the prayer was not as easy. It tormented me. What were we going to tell those who would join us? I didn't want it to be political or sound judgmental.

All night long, I began the phrase "pray for… " repeatedly to myself, but could not think of any words to finish it.

Finally, the voice that easily answered the first two

questions broke through again: *Stop thinking and let go.*

I didn't respond. The advice was sound.

Darn it.

"Letting go. Okay. I'm letting go," I mumbled to myself as I adjusted my CPAP mask and tried to breathe.

"Pray for… Pray for…"

Pray for what? the voice interrupted. *Just say it.*

I hated that voice.

"Pray for Phil!" I blurted into my mask.

I bolted upright. Next to me, Diane grunted and turned over.

"'Pray for Phil?' Where did that come from?" I whispered to the dark.

I knew, but didn't want to admit it.

"That makes no sense," I argued with the night. "Phil who? I know a lot of Phils. Relatives, friends, students…"

Not Phil the who, but PHIL the what.

"Huh?"

PHIL is an acronym.

My mind began to clear. "Ah, acronym. Of course. Diane loves acronyms. But what is PHIL?"

What four things does DC need that begin with the letters P, H, I, and L?

The words came faster than I could think them. "Peace, hope, integrity, love."

Good, the voice said.

It couldn't be that easy.

"No, not good," I argued, reverting to my English teacher mode. "We need parallelism. *Peace*, *hope*, and *love* are fine. They all have one syllable. *Integrity* has four. What *I* word that DC needs has only one syllable?"

In the dark, I saw a frustrated face grimace in frustration.

This isn't poetry. Integrity is what we need. It's fine. Go with the word. 'Praying for PHIL in DC.' That's what you're going to do. Tell your wife.

"You want me to wake her?"

You can tell her in the morning.

The next day, I rose early and sat in front of my computer downstairs to make a simple Facebook ad—a picture of the Capitol, "Pray for PHIL" in a common font, date and time. It looked okay, but only okay. I edited, rearranged, lightened here, darkened there until I was satisfied, then emailed the finished product to Diane's computer in the office.

She was already up, working.

"I like it," she answered, with a smile emoji.

I liked it too. Simple. Open. Not political. Not judgmental.

Just the way PHIL would want it, I thought, giving the voice a name.

I smiled, copied the image to Facebook and pushed *Send*. We were ready to go.

The voice was silent until the night before we left for Washington. Neither Diane nor I slept well. She had a persistent cough and left our room, evidently to leave me alone with the familiar voice.

Nice job with the ad, PHIL said. *Now let's talk about the book.*

"Book? What book?"

There was always going to be a book. Didn't I tell you? For those who didn't hear about the walk in time. What's the problem? You've written books before.

"Sure. *Horror* books."

That's not the point. You have stories to tell, stories to help others, stories of finding PHIL.

"Finding PHIL... you're PHIL."

This time.

"And others."

Yes, but you've had lots of PHILs. That's what I want you to tell. All the times PHIL in whatever form has spoken and helped in your life. You have lots of material.

"Are you saying I'm old?"

...You have lots of material.

I sat alone in bed, conjuring reasons to say no.

After minutes of silence, the voice spoke again. *You*

remember that time your sister told your parents to color Easter eggs at Christmas time?

I reluctantly smiled remembering an adamant four-year-old stomping her feet, grabbing my mother's hand, and tugging her toward the kitchen. Her words echoed in the night. I nodded.

What did she say?

"Do it, sweetie," I said.

And so?

I sighed and rested my head on the wall. "I guess I'm writing a book."

So here I am, telling you how PHIL—the four traits of peace, hope, integrity, and love— help conquer the chaos of living. The stories are true—mostly. The people are real—mostly.

That said, this is what some people call *creative non-fiction.* To protect the privacy of the people and places involved, I've altered many names and locations. In some instances, events have been enhanced to illustrate the lessons learned from them, which makes them truer for more people than just me.

Concerning the arrangement of the events, chronology has been ignored. Why? Because finding the traits of peace, hope, integrity, and love is a lifelong search, and sometimes the events that illustrate them don't occur in the same order acronym letters do, which is okay. What's important is that they do occur and we learn from them.

The most significant truth I learned relating these tales is that with PHIL—in the form of many people, voices, situations, facial expressions, and memories—we can weather almost anything, be it the social distancing of a mass quarantine or even high school English. By finding, embracing, and enriching these four traits of our personalities, we can and will conquer chaos.

Peace

Pivotal Decisions

"FIVE ENEMIES OF PEACE inhabit with us - avarice, ambition, envy, anger, and pride; if these were to be banished, we should infallibly enjoy perpetual peace."
Petrarch

For most people, high school senior year is a pivotal experience. No more dilly-dallying. It's time to get off the couch and decide what you are going to do with the rest of your life. Call it graduation or a rite of passage or parental relief, it's been the same for a long time.

My problem was I didn't want to leave. I really liked learning. I liked my teachers. I loved my classes. (Well, other than phy ed. and shop) I didn't want it to be over.

However, without the requisite superpowers, I couldn't stop time. The end was near. As I removed the pages from my 1969 calendar, June loomed large ahead. Decisions had to be made.

I had already applied for and been admitted to the Institute of Technology at the University of Minnesota. Why did I apply to that school when Bemidji State was just down the road? Because engineers made better money and there would always be a future for them. Teachers, counselors, friends, and parents all told me this, and I believed them.

A conflict loomed, however, because of my weekend

work on a survey crew. From those weekends slogging through swamps, snowdrifts, and gravel pits; after cutting line and running levels in all sorts of weather; and after dodging traffic and angry geese, I had also decided that civil engineering—the career that had been mapped out for me—wasn't going to work.

Oh, I could do it. I just hated it.

Besides, there were other alternatives. Since the advent of the space program, news reports had extolled the future of these new-fangled machines called *computers*, and they looked cool on television. Sparkling, tall, metal boxes with lights and tape spools, stacks of cards feeding them, quick answers to long questions…

And SPACE! I loved everything outer space—stars, rockets, the moon, Mars. I knew I could never be an astronaut because of my glasses, but computers could involve me in the program. How neat would that be?

Another positive aspect of this new technology was being on the ground floor. Anything I invented, developed, or discovered beyond the task at hand was bound to bring accolades and fame. That should make everybody happy.

A major downside, however, was that having lived most of my life in the north woods of Minnesota, I had never seen a computer in real-life. Just pictures in a *Popular Science* magazine.

Then there was the whole math thing. Colleges and scientists said you had to be good at math. I kind of was, but I would much rather determine the guitar chords of a Beatles song than understand the practical uses of the quadratic formula.

But the computer field was engineering of a sort and it was work. It didn't have to be fun. It just had to make me and my parents happy. The best part was it could make me rich.

Then there was this persistent thought running through my brain that said, *You know what would make you really happy? Music. And your guitar. Just look what it did for Bob Dylan and he grew up in northern Minnesota, too. Hibbing! You could do that.*

I knew that would never fly.

"Music is too iffy. Too many variables. Too much competition. You're too smart to take chances like that," my parents always said...although I had never even mentioned the idea to them.

So I decided to suck it up, and off to the university I went, intent on a lucrative career in this new field called computer engineering. I was excited, confident, and totally naïve. My first week of class changed all that. Reality struck like a fastball to the face, upsetting my career path.

Discovery number one: Calculus, the mathematical foundation of engineering no matter which field you were in, was not just advanced math which I had squeaked through in high school; it was a foreign universe.

Discovery number two: Fortran computer language, the driving force behind computer calculations, was not the same as English, Spanish, or even Klingon. I couldn't even understand the textbook's table of contents.

Discovery number three: Even what I was good at was still lousy. On the first day of Freshman English, the teacher gave an in-class essay. On the second day, she handed back the paper face down on my desk, announcing I had the second highest grade in the class. Grinning widely, I turned over the essay. D+.

Discovery number four: This was not going to be easy or fun. I didn't know anything about computers or anything. I also found myself envious of everybody who did. Clearly, computers were not for me, either talent-wise or interest level. On the positive side, I did excel in an upper division music class on Gregorian chants.

Exactly how I could use that skill in computers was not clear.

Just weeks into college life, it was time to reevaluate my goals. What did I really want?

That had not really changed. I wanted money, success, and recognition for my achievements (such as they would be). Therefore, engineering was still the way to go. I knew that. I believed that.

Just not computers or civil engineering, which meant I had to find something interesting. Something that inspired me.

Walking to class on Engineering Row one day, I discovered the perfect answer: architecture.

Of course!

I loved buildings—seeing them transform from a hole in the ground to a work of art and functionality. I marveled at their design, their construction, their variety. Everything from libraries to stadiums to factories. I mean, just look at the buildings on campus from the classicism of the East Bank to the Modernity of the West Bank. The variety. The invention. The design.

Architecture. The perfect major.

I immediately looked up the courses in the school catalogue and loved the curriculum. This was it!

I forgot what I didn't know—calculus, art, history.

Two other issues also dampened my enthusiasm. First, looming over any change of plans was the military draft which could select me at any moment, thrust me into uniform, and ship me off to Vietnam. Changing majors would increase that possibility. Secondly, I still liked music.

"No," I decided. "I'm not Dylan. Besides, as he said, 'The times they are a'changin'.' I'm going to be an architect. I can do this."

No, I couldn't.

I was no better at architecture than I was with computers. One plus was I enjoyed my classes, especially in architectural history. I couldn't draw and I knew nothing about construction, but I still loved what I was learning. When my advisor told me I might do better in another profession, I was not surprised, just disappointed.

Voices galore—both external and internal—told me I needed a major redirection, but the U was too expensive to explore my options. Even though it would disappoint my parents and high school teachers, I decided to go back home and attend Bemidji State until I could figure out what to do.

Foolishly, because the degree was always marketable, I tried the math route, only to have my previous disinterest confirmed. Then I thought, *I was pretty good at architectural history…. history. Yeah. What about history?*

A friend asked, "What do you do with a history major?"

"That's easy," I answered. "Teach."

"Do you really want to teach?"

That question halted my eagerness. I remembered the old adage "Those who can, do. Those who can't, teach." Despite the insult, a degree would settle me down and get me out working.

At least, for a while.

I was young. I could always change.

My new Bemidji advisor encouraged me to try it, with the suggestion to expand my major beyond the specific application of history to the general discipline of social studies, which consisted of government, geography, economics, sociology, psychology, philosophy, and history. Like a chocoholic leaping eagerly into a sea of Jello pudding, I followed his suggestion.

The variety and interaction of the courses, the way each one built on the others—I loved it! I could spend a lifetime learning this.

And not just learning it, I realized, but teaching it. I thought back to all the instructors I had known and realized teaching may not pay well, but it was a people profession. It wasn't just work. You explored places and ideas, values and life itself. Instead of competing with people, you helped them.

Yeah.

Teaching.

It was worth a shot.

So I took the bachelor of science classes. I learned about human growth and development. I even took the required five credits of physical education and survived them. Because

I needed a minor, I utilized my U of M engineering classes for one in junior high physics.

And just when I felt confident and secure in my future, as I had feared, the military called.

So now I'm supposed to be a soldier? Really?

"You do what you have to do," my parents told me.

Dutifully, I took my draft physical and passed. I received the letter classifying me *1A*. I prepared to go when the call came.

It never did.

The month I anticipated my induction, the lottery numbers dropped below mine. Two months later, the draft ended entirely.

Now what? I wondered.

You wanted to be a teacher. Be a teacher, came the answer.

So I did. I finished the course work. I immersed myself in student teaching and understood something as important as what brought me to Bemidji State: I liked music, sure, but I *loved* this profession!

Getting a job, however, was going to be a problem. A quick review of teacher openings throughout Minnesota revealed that social studies positions required an extracurricular assignment.

Most often a sports coach.

Most commonly football.

My problem was I was short, scrawny, and the size of a football.

After numerous rejections, I realized through no fault of my own, social studies wasn't going to work, but I still wanted to teach. I looked through the listings for a companion major that would complement social studies, one that would increase my chances of finding work. The certification listed most often was English.

How long would that take? I thought.

According to the Bemidji State catalogue, I could complete that degree in one year.

I'll do it, I resolved, which was the right decision. When I finished my course work that following summer, three English openings became available in the school where I had student taught.

Recalling all the voices, I concluded that evidently I was supposed to be an English teacher.

Decades later, my search, my experience, and PHIL taught me an even more important lesson: Money is a horrible motivator. So are the fame, competition, pride, and anger that accompany it.

In the pivotal moments of life, rather than selfish battles with things like calculus, construction codes, or Fortran, we need to find a poetic, scholarly, almost Petrarchan peace by banishing the obstructions and learn to help others. In other words, stop fighting for status and stuff. Enjoy what is and who you are.

PHIL says.

The Presence of Everything

"PEACE IS THE BEAUTY of life. It is sunshine. It is the smile of a child, the love of a mother, the joy of a father, the togetherness of a family. It is the advancement of man, the victory of a just cause, the triumph of truth."
Menachem Begin

I don't know if it was growing up in the woods, the side effects of the 60s, or an aberrant philosophical gene of adolescence, but my high school friends and I liked to discuss things beyond football, parties, and music. We liked to think. Even though we were just learning how.

That didn't matter. We had a lot to think about—beliefs, concepts, and principles we could understand no better than we could understand the sudden appearance of facial hair, burgeoning body parts, and acne. Things were happening around us and to us.

There were assassinations—John Kennedy, Malcolm X, Martin Luther King Jr, Robert Kennedy. There was war. There was a sexual revolution. There was psychedelia. There was the Jesus Movement. In reality, we knew nothing, but we pretended we had all the answers our parents wouldn't teach us.

However, satisfactory explanations and solutions to the madness of the world proved elusive. We looked for them everywhere. We read poetry and books. We listened to speakers, thinkers and singers while we mourned the death of friends and family.

Left with no certainties, we rebelled. Frustrated by the television fluff that ignored reality, we turned from slapstick to satire. Resenting the triteness of bubble gum radio, we rejected "Yummy Yummy" and "Sugar Sugar" in favor of *Sgt. Pepper* and "Pinball Wizard." Discouraged by fairy tale endings that never came true, we abandoned Disney for *Easy Rider*.

Life was not as we imagined it would be. Our grandparents and parents had survived the Great Depression and World War II, believing they would leave us a better life —calmer, more stable, happier. Something went horribly awry and had to change some way somehow. As a generation, we resolved to find it.

One night in a college dorm, months after John and Yoko sang "Give Peace a Chance" and after the three days of Woodstock, a roomful of us spent the evening discussing the military draft and the university's ROTC (Reserve Officer Training Corps) program. Cary, one of boys, claimed irrefutable expertise by holding up the peace symbol hanging around his neck and announcing, "If they call me, I'm not going. This is what the world needs more than dead bodies."

"Peace?"

"Yep."

Jennifer, a girl in the corner with a soft voice and tired eyes, asked innocently, "What is peace?"

The silence that followed was telling.

Cary scratched his head and ventured, "The absence of war."

The room groaned. Even as teenagers, we knew that was crazy. Wars never stopped. Throughout history, one always followed another. For example, WWI led to WWII, which led to Korea, which led to Vietnam.

And those were just the latest American wars. What about all those raging across Africa, the Middle East, and South America that the US had nothing to do with? If "absence of war" were the definition, peace was impossible.

Besides, what was war? It wasn't just military battles. Back in the boonies where most of us grew up, far from the battlefields and air strikes, there were clashes between religions, races, and married couples. Wherever you turned, you found conflict piled upon conflict. Maybe no tanks tearing up the fields and B52s thundering across the sky, but nothing you could call peace either. Every day, hostility provoked confrontation which caused injury and destruction. Nobody was immune from this anti-peace.

Jennifer pushed back her long hair and summed up the truth none of us wanted to acknowledge: "Peace is not an absence of anything; peace is an illusion."

I wanted to forget her words as soon as she said them, but life would not let me. Throughout the 70s, Jennifer's conclusion proved more and more accurate. Across the globe, crisis led to crisis. Worldwide, one assassination built on another. In Ohio and Mississippi, soldiers and police killed college students. In Washington, DC, the Watergate scandal ripped apart the nation. Long after we lost track of Jennifer, her words reverberated in our brains: "Peace is an illusion."

None of us still had any idea what it was.

Then, for just one second, we caught a glimpse from an improbable source.

Menachem Begin.

We Americans first heard of him years before as an Israeli militant leader, most often for his violent acts. Even those who supported Israel and agreed with its goals recognized him as a lightning rod for combat and bloodshed. In fact, many of us considered him the embodiment of war.

Then, one day in 1977, the universe shuddered.

Begin became Israeli prime minister.

We were terrified.

What atrocities he would commit with such power?

Israel was surrounded by enemies. Who would he attack first? And the danger was not just in the Middle East. Armageddon threatened us all.

However, instead of inciting World War III and the destruction of the universe, two years after his ascension to his new office, Begin appeared on television, standing next to Israel's chief rival, Egyptian president Anwar Sadat, as well as American president Jimmy Carter. Together, they announced the Camp David Accords to end the fighting between Israel and Egypt. Suddenly, rather than one of the Four Horsemen of the Apocalypse, Begin transformed to an agent of reconciliation, earning him and Sadat the Nobel Peace Prize.

The world was stunned.

Whether or not you called his conversion a miracle, an epiphany, or a strange case of indigestion, obviously something phenomenal had happened inside this man, if only for the moments he delivered his Nobel speech. His words resounded throughout the world to those most in need of hearing them.

Even in backwoods Minnesota.

I remember thinking as I watched the news reports, *I hope whatever happened to him happens to me and all of us in that U of M dorm room.*

I hoped we all perceived the reality that peace does indeed exist, not as Cary's *absence of war* nor as Jennifer's *illusion*, but as Begin explained so eloquently "…the beauty of life….sunshine….the smile of a child, the love of a mother, the joy of a father, the togetherness of a family…. the advancement of man, the victory of a just cause, the triumph of truth."

Or as PHIL revealed, "Peace is the presence of everything. The trick is to notice and embrace it."

Smiling Norville

"PEACE BEGINS WITH A smile."
Mother Teresa

The day I moved into my new house in the Twin Cites, I had an idea.

A good idea.

A life-changing idea.

Not one of those hare-brained concepts that fall apart after about two minutes of flash and frustration. Something to alleviate the lonely hours of adjusting to a new environment. Something that would allow me to utilize my skills and interests. Something that could keep me focused for hours at a time with the promise of fame and fortune. Something fun.

I would write a book.

No. More than a "book."

A novel.

After years of correcting student writing, after reading hundreds of professionally-written stories and critical essays, after gagging on pages of hopelessly feeble description and cliché-ridden dialogue, it was time to step forward and show everybody how writing is supposed to be done. Nothing fancy with even a knee-deep theme. Something light, like a sappy little love story. Entertaining, but still good.

Idea after idea popped into my brain. I was excited.

The subject outline quickly took shape: A rural high school principal dreams of escaping to Hollywood and becoming a screenwriter. While watching the Academy Awards, he falls madly in love with the woman who wins that year's Best Original Screenplay award.

There! In two sentences, I had setting. I had a protagonist. I had conflict. Humorous situations were sure to come. I could build on that.

That's enough, I thought. *Time to get started.*

Oh, I was diligent. Since I was on vacation and work was still weeks away, I sat down at my computer and typed furiously. Words flowed onto the screen. Hour after hour, they kept coming. Each incident led to another. Each comic barb resulted in silliness and slapstick. Page built upon page. I was on a roll.

I loved it. The process. The result. All of it. No doubt, this was going to be great.

I had to brag to somebody, so I called my sister Amy, a fellow English major, but with the added experience of being a free-lance writer. As all good siblings should, she was very supportive, but after I described the plot and where I was in the process, she suggested I get feedback from another voice, an unbiased opinion, maybe a writing coach, to give me an objective reaction.

"Do you know anybody?" I asked.

'Well, yeah. I can give him your name if you want."

"Yeah, that would be great."

Two days later I received a phone call. The name—Norville Dowd—and words he used were accented—British? Maybe?—but he sounded enthusiastic about seeing my work.

"How much do you have so far?" he asked.

"I guess about 75 pages. Is that too much?"

"No, no. That's fine. Send them and I'll get back to you."

That was all I needed to hear. I printed off what I had, stuffed all 75 pages plus a cover letter into a large envelope, sent them across the city, and waited.

And waited.

And waited.

This was not going as I had planned. How long could it take to read anyway? I called my sister and asked her.

"Well, he does have other clients," she reminded me. "Give him a few weeks. It will be fine."

Weeks? WEEKS? How could it take weeks? It only took days to write what I sent him.

Of course, she was right, but I didn't want to admit it.

Calm down, Frickstad. It will be fine.

Of course, it would. As soon as he read it, he would find me an agent. I would get a call and my new career would begin in earnest. Who needed teaching anyway? This would be great.

Every spare moment, I built my expectations. I began making plans of what to do with the millions I was going to make.

Finally, the call came.

"Mike. Norville Dowd here. I read your book. I'd really like to talk about it. Can you meet me Thursday this week?"

Can I meet you this week? YES! Of course. Yes.

After agreeing on the place and time, I paced my house. He really hadn't said anything about the book, but he had called back, so that must be good. Right?

Of course, right. I wandered from room to room, up and down the stairs, playing and replaying the humility I would show at our meeting.

Yes, thank you very much. I don't know where the idea came from, but...Groundbreaking? Well, I wouldn't say... Really? A best-seller? Wow!

Taking deep breaths and pumping my arms as I bounced through the house, I talked to myself. "He wants to talk about my book. And he doesn't even know me. I'm going to be rich!"

Day after day, I talked and talked and talked, convincing myself of my talent. Finally, Thursday came. Claiming my 60s heritage by wearing a psychedelic tie designed by

Grateful Dead icon Jerry Garcia, I strutted to my car, cranked up the Classic Rock FM station, and drove across town. In a quiet, tree-lined, Minneapolis neighborhood, I parked in front of an inauspicious house.

This was the place. Looking into the future, I saw a historical marker next to the door: "On this site, esteemed author Michael Frickstad launched his writing career."

I smiled, switched off the engine, and opened the door.

The swagger only lasted until I tried to stand up. My knees buckled. My hands sweat. My breath caught. The poise and self-assurance that drove me across the metro faltered.

"No, no, no. No fear. You can do this," I reassured myself.

I grabbed a notebook to record all the compliments Norville would surely give, and I wobbled to the door.

Okay. Small porch. One step up. I can do this.

I stood on the square, concrete platform a moment, inhaled deeply, and pushed the doorbell.

Nobody answered.

Inside, there were no thumping footsteps. No barking dog. Nothing.

I rang the doorbell again. I heard it ring. Still no response.

Was this the right day? Was this the wrong house?

I turned back to the car to check.

"Hallo!" a voice called from inside. Swiveling back to the house, I nearly tripped myself as the door opened revealing a tall, balding man dressed in shorts, a t-shirt, and sandals. "You must be Mike. I'm Norville," he said, his smile gleaming through the screen door. "Come in."

He ushered me into the living room, explaining, "I was just finishing up some notes on another project. I'll be right back. You okay? You need anything to drink? Water? Juice?"

His smile erased my nervousness.

"No. I'm fine."

In a second, he returned, carrying the envelope I had sent him, the top split open.

He read it, I thought. *This is going to be so good. I wonder what he liked best? The characters? The description? The dialogue?*

His happy, relaxed posture as he sat opposite me relieved my tension, except I thought his bare legs clashed with my slacks and tie. My grin twitched and shuddered as I flipped quickly through my notebook for an empty page. With the paper finally smoothed and ready, I clicked my pen. I exhaled and announced, "Okay. I'm ready."

Norville pulled out the manuscript and laid it on the coffee table in front of us. On top of it was a page of typed notes. He beamed positivity.

A page of compliments, I thought. *Where is he going to start?*

"I just have to say," he declared, "this really sucks."

My pen fell from my fingers and rattled across the coffee table.

Sucks? Wha– No, that can't be right.

My mouth quaked and grimaced. I gagged on the air.

"I know that's not what you wanted to hear, but I made some comments here," Norville said. "Let me explain what I mean."

My hands scrambled across the table to retrieve my pen. The room tilted. Did he say *sucked*? Really? Why was he smiling? I was paying him for this?

What a jerk! I should run outside and ram my car into his house. I should—

Then I listened to his words. He wasn't attacking me; he was helping me, pointing out deficiencies, blatant clichés I had ignored, and haunting improbabilities, each correction accompanied with a comforting "See?" and an encouraging grin.

This wasn't just a consultation. I was living the other side of every classroom in which I had ever worked. This time, however, I was the student and this stranger was my teacher. I recognized everything he said. I used every phrase myself.

Well, not *sucked*, but I wanted to many times. MANY times.

The same words that just destroyed my imaginary world

Norville meant to soothe rather than embroil, to repair my work rather than destroy, to bring peace rather than disappointment.

Besides, he was right: Despite what I thought as I wrote those pages, they really did suck. All was not lost, however. His smile reassured me I could fix this.

Funny thing, smiles.

As Mother Teresa suggested, "Peace begins with a smile." They are the ultimate peacemaker, whether from a friend or a stranger. They lighten the mood of the smiler, the "smilee," and anybody nearby. They erase pain. They accept the unaccepted. By lifting anger, fear, and abandonment, they turn the grumpiest curmudgeon into a giggly urchin.

Most importantly for writers, they turn discouragement into inspiration.

When I got home from that business conference, those 75 pages of *suck* transformed into a twelve-year project of writing, revising, editing, reimagining, rewriting, re-revising, re-editing… eventually converting my "sappy little love story" into a novel.

And another novel.

And this.

So what if my work never became best sellers with millions of dollars in movie rights and an on-going franchise? So what if Norville still thought my books sucked? He taught me a great PHIL lesson that day: Peace not only begins with a smile; it endures with a smile. No matter if I make a million dollars or 99¢. I am at peace with that. I'll keep smiling.

The Wrong You Can Live With

"WHEN THE POWER OF love overcomes the love of power, the world will know peace."
Jimi Hendrix

When I recently found the words "When the power of love overcomes the love of power, the world will know peace" attributed to rock guitar legend Jimi Hendrix, my initial reaction was "Hendrix didn't say that!"

But as soon as I thought it, I wished he had. I wanted to believe that truth can alter people's awareness and search for peace. Even that of a drug-addled rocker.

I later read the original speaker was more likely William Gladstone, 19th century prime minister of the United Kingdom. Another source credited Sri Chimnoy, a 20th century Indian spiritual leader and teacher of meditation.

"Who cares?" I grumbled. "The words are accurate. I've seen them come true."

I didn't care to reflect on how I understood that reality. In fact, I avoided why. My point was the source is not as important as what the words say: Peace comes from love, not from power, whether in international relations or personal interactions.

Even in cases of divorce.

The sink rattled with one small pot, one plate, one fork and spoon, and one plastic drinking glass.

Looking out the kitchen window, I watched the vacant alley across the yard as the sun set behind the trees. Grass grew between the tire tracks from lack of use. I sighed, then glanced behind myself at the flat, shiny table; the two empty chairs; and the blank kitchen.

No pictures on the wall. No refrigerator magnets. No life.
That's depressing.

Returning my attention to the sink, I rinsed the few dishes and the empty can of SpaghettiOs. There was no dish towel, so I wiped my hands on my pants and left everything to dry in the sink.

On my way across the room, I noticed the stove clock read 6:30. Too early for bed.
Couldn't sleep anyway.

Sleep hadn't come easily forever.

I switched off the kitchen light and let my stockinged feet slide across the kitchen, dining room, and into the living room.

There wasn't a whole lot to occupy me there either, but there was a television. One of the few things that remained after my wife had left.

That and my record collection. I snorted and grumbled, "All records but no stereo."

"Later," she had said.

When we still talked.

I turned on the television and flipped through the few channels the town received from Fargo. The news shows were over and there was still a half hour before prime time began.

Agitated, I switched off the tv and plopped into the easy chair next to the pole lamp. Alternately, I stared at the light switch on the pole and my empty hand. Finally, I sighed and laid my head back on the chair. With nothing to watch, nothing to read, and nothing to do, I sat alone in the dim light.

I didn't move. I didn't think. I just sat, feeling lost and overwhelmed.

How long had they been gone? My wife and son. I couldn't remember.

Months? No. More than months.

Years? Could it really be that long?

No, it couldn't, I argued, but when I flipped through my mind for dates, I realized it had to be. I scratched my head and scowled.

Did it really matter? Even it did, what was I going to do about it? Probably nothing. I was good at doing nothing.

The doorbell rang, jarring me awake. I gripped the chair arms and raised my head.

I hadn't heard that sound in a long time. People didn't just drop over anymore. Grumbling, I pushed my way up, shuffled into the front hall, snapped on the porch light, and opened the door. The man wearing a clerical collar surprised me.

My minister.

My wife's boss.

I unlocked the screen door and pushed it open. "Pastor?" I asked "What's going on?"

"Hi, Mike. Can we talk?"

"Uh…yeah. Sure."

I didn't think I had talked to the pastor outside of church ever. I ushered him into the living room, offering a seat on the couch while I returned to the easy chair.

We both sat uncomfortably, avoiding each other's eyes, silently daring the other to begin.

Reluctantly, I finally asked, "What did you want to talk about?"

The minister leaned over his knees, scrunched his lips, then said, "I think you know."

I sat back in my chair, my hands clasping the arms, my eyes locked on the carpet in front of me.

"How long can this go on?" he asked.

I shook my head. "I don't know. She's the one who left and took—"

I choked back the tears and halted. Finally, I whispered, "Sorry. I just— just— I want them back. They have to come back."

The pastor held his hands together and nodded. "Do you ever see that happening?"

I sat back and gazed into the darkness outside. I recalled the day I came home to an empty bedroom. I relived the night of accusations, revelations, and slamming doors. Once more, I heard the anger, tasted the tears, felt the hollow futility. My aching arms trembled from the pain of hugging my son goodbye.

I knew the truth. My wife and son were gone for good. Yes, only across town, but they were gone. They weren't coming back and there was nothing I could do about it.

I nervously licked my lips, glanced at the pastor, and shook my head."

He leaned forward, his hand on my shoulder. "Then you have to let them go.

I gazed at the stiff white collar. "How can you say that?" I challenged. "You're a minister. Divorce is wrong."

"It is, but a wise person once told me that life doesn't always give you a choice between right and wrong. Sometimes your only choices are between two wrongs."

I hated those words. I had heard them before. "Who told you that?" I grumbled.

"You did."

I sighed. Of course, I did. Years before this man came to town, his predecessor told them to me. In another situations in a different lifetime, I repeated them often to conflicted friends struggling with life's trials. Now they came back to convict me.

The pastor continued. "This isn't good for either you or her, and it's definitely not good for your son. What you went through before she left was bad enough, don't you think?"

I laughed and nodded. "Oh, yeah."

"Well, as bad as it was, at least the three of you shared your lives back then. You worked through things as well as you could. Somehow that all changed and it's still changing. Right now, there is no *you* together. Right now, all you two do is struggle for power, which only makes life worse, driving you further apart."

"So you're saying divorce is the answer?"

Reluctantly, he nodded at me. "As bad as divorce is, sometimes it's better just to stop. Stop all the fighting, all the hurting, all the retaliation. If there was ever any love between you, now is the time to give up the scramble for control and love each other enough to just… just walk away."

I sucked my lower lip as I realized the truth.

Peace is more important than winning. Besides, we've both already lost.

I nodded.

"I can tell her it's final then?" the pastor asked.

"Yeah," I whispered as I wiped a tear from my cheek.

"And you'll tell her, too?"

The running tears would not stop. I wiped them from my chin with my sleeve. The pastor took my hands and prayed. I didn't understand the words. Later, I just remembered him standing, rubbing my shoulder, and walking out the front door.

As I stated earlier, whoever first said "When the power of love overcomes the love of power, the world will know peace" doesn't matter. Let it be Gladstone. Let it be Chimnoy. Heck, let it be Hendrix. In today's world, what matters is their accuracy.

For millennia we've believed the power of love binds people together in marriage, while the love of power breaks that bond in divorce. However, sometimes the only way the power of love can overcome the love of power is by untying the marriage knot. Why? Because love seeks peace, and sometimes the only means of achieving it is by loving someone enough to let them go.

Even though it hurts.

Even though it's "wrong."

Especially if, as PHIL says, the power of love is the only "wrong" you can live with.

A Stone's Throw

"WHEN YOU'VE SEEN BEYOND yourself, then you may find, peace of mind is waiting there."
George Harrison

It had been a tumultuous year.

Health issues. Physical and occupational therapy. Retirement. Lost relationships.

But I was okay. I had my family. I had my house. I had my mind. I had my finances. I was even meeting my physical goals. My therapists and doctors encouraged me that life would improve, and I held onto their words. I was content.

Maybe not deliriously happy, but content.

Then I met this woman at the library.

We didn't talk a lot at first, mainly texting and Facebook conversations. I accepted that. My heart was safer that way.

However, I could not get past the notion we should never have met and yet for some reason we had. We lived on opposite sides of the city. We traveled in two different ethnic and religious circles. I was older. Given those differences, a second look felt both foolish and dangerous. Still, our encounter and social interaction also seemed significant to both of us, as if something or someone had introduced us for a crucial reason.

We agreed to meet again. This time, we would avoid the

cliché of meeting in the library, opting instead for a café.

In a Barnes and Noble bookstore.

As usual, I arrived early, giving me time to analyze the situation. We had been texting for over a week now, sending short, safe, and superficial messages that were still innocently probing. Probably too safe. Even though this would be the second time we had met in person and we had exchanged daily texts, we didn't really know anything about each other. But I sensed we wanted to.

At least I did, and after all I had been through in the last year, everything was about me! So I carefully planned the evening's conversation.

At our initial meeting, I had explained my medical history—primarily my stroke and recovery—but we had glossed over the simple introductory material people usually discuss, like where we were from, how many kids do we have, what do we like to do for fun, and do we like to travel. In other words, the basics. Tonight, I was determined to delve deeper into our past—at least hers.

That was my plan.

I would tell something about myself; she would answer with something about herself. Before long, I'd know if there was any reason to continue with this relationship.

That's not how the evening progressed.

Oh, we talked. I revealed a lot of my past, my jobs, my goals. She talked about cooking, books, work. The conversation was friendly, even relaxed. However, it soon became clear we were avoiding something important, something big. I didn't know what that could be, but I was pretty sure it had something to do with her. Other than an elevated ego, I was perfect.

After wracking my brain how to approach the subject, I blurted out what I thought was a simple question that would clear up everything: "So… what's your story?"

Which was obviously the *wrong* question.

I wouldn't say she blanched, but she definitely hesitated. Her eyes examined my face as she clasped her coffee cup in both hands. Finally, she looked aside and said, "I'm not ready to go there yet."

She could have walked away—and I half-expected her to, but she didn't. Instead, she looked back at me and asked, "Okay?"

Which told me there was a story she needed to tell. Just later.

And it was a story I needed to hear, but not to satisfy my own curiosity. What I needed to hear was beyond me, beyond any possible us. Something difficult had happened to her, but exactly what didn't matter. What was important was how she dealt with the circumstances and how she found peace with them.

So I waited.

A week and a half later, we met again. Before I could develop a strategy to approach the issue again, she jumped right into the subject.

"Your question really unnerved me," she told me.

"I didn't mean to pry. I just—"

"I know. And someday I'll tell you. I'm working on it. One step at a time."

"Steps?"

She nodded. "Isn't that what we're going through, steps?"

I sat back and nodded as well. "I guess."

"The first one...was the biggest, and so was you asking me my story. I'm not ready to tell it, but I really think it helped that you asked."

I wanted to ask how it helped not to answer, but I wasn't going to wreck the moment. I sat quietly, waiting, hoping she'd explain. Finally, as if she heard my thoughts, she leaned over the table and said, "The reason I didn't want to tell the story is because I threw it all away."

"Threw it away?"

She nodded. "I was having a hard time, as you can probably tell. I had to get away from Minnesota, so I called a friend on the East Coast and asked if I could come visit. After hanging listlessly around her house for a while, I decided to go to the ocean. Have you ever been to the ocean?"

"Sure."

"There's something about the smell, the sound of the waves. And it's so big. Yet it's still so peaceful. You know?"

"Uh-huh," I replied, despite images of hurricanes, undertows, and sharks running through my brain.

She continued, "So I was standing next to the water, and I picked up this rock. Nothing unique. Just a normal rock. I held it in my hand and looked at it while I thought about… thought about everything that had happened. And then I said to it, 'You. You are my story,' and I threw it as hard as I could into the ocean.

"I know it sounds silly, but it felt so good. All the tears, all the hurt, everything bad was just gone, swallowed up in one splash.

"That's why I don't want to talk about it. I threw everything away. That story is done. I'm starting over. Okay?"

That's why the ocean—I get it now.

"You want peace," I said. "You're looking beyond."

"Right. At least for a while. Is that okay?"

"Yes. I still want to know, but…Yes. It's okay."

Her hand touched mine. "Oh, I'll explain it all someday," she said. "If you can just hang on for a little while…"

I looked down at our hands as I reflected on my past year. They belonged together.

Then I looked up and examined her face. In her eyes, I saw what she had seen in the ocean: peace and promise.

In that second, I was more than content. I was happy.

I hung on.

Days turned into weeks, weeks into months, as we discovered what was important to both of us—laughter, joy, discovery, relationship, and finding goodness and God in everything and everybody. Together, we laughed and cried. Together, we sang and prayed. Together, we found family. Bit by bit, both our stories revealed themselves and merged into a new story all our own.

We married.

As months turned into years, we learned much about the peace the world is searching for. It is not simply enduring and gritting our teeth in anger at somebody we really want to smack upside the head. It is not clutching to remnants of the past. It is instead loving our existence right now. It is embracing satisfaction and the uniqueness that is every human being around us. It is playing with our grandchildren. It is sharing a seat on a bus. It is the security of thought, the safety to be and do what we want. It is the freedom to be what we were always meant to be.

It is the lesson of PHIL we all need to hear: Anything that is not peace—anger, fear, sorrow, turmoil—is a stone to be thrown into the ocean.

Hope

Better Things to Do

"HOPE BEGINS IN THE dark, the stubborn hope that if you just show up and try to do the right thing, the dawn will come. You wait and watch and work: you don't give up."
Anne Lamott

Nobody ever accomplished anything by giving up. By trying something else, yes, but giving up, never.

Growing up, I had this bizarre goal of becoming a professional athlete. It didn't matter what kind. Baseball, football, basketball—any activity that included a spheroid accompanied by running, jumping, throwing, kicking, or hitting. My biggest obstacle to success was a congenital tendency to use the wrong skill for the wrong sport. Just so you know, kicking a baseball is not recommended, nor is hitting a basketball or dribbling a football.

Even then, PHIL told me, although I refused to listen, "Really, there are better things you could be doing. You may have won a football in the local Punt, Pass, and Kick contest, but seriously. That's enough. Try something else."

"No, no, I can do this," I protested before increasing my futile attempts.

With every failure, the admonitions continued: "Listen. I understand. Hope is a great thing, but you're hoping for the wrong thing. Have you thought about knitting? Please. It's okay."

To reinforce PHIL's advice, not only did my abilities fail me, my clumsiness generated more pain: a baseball to the side of the head, a knee to a concrete wall, a ping pong table to the groin.

But I still hoped things would change, that with enough practice, skill would triumph and someone somewhere would recognize the innate athletic talent that inhabited my body. Through it all, PHIL's warned me to occupy my time elsewhere.

Then my folly received support from an unexpected advocate: Bemidji State College.

As mentioned earlier, a Minnesota teaching license required the completion of five quarter credits of physical education classes.

Ha! I thought. *No counseling friends, no parental pleading, no nagging inner voice can change an institutional mandate.*

And I didn't want them to. Just the prospect of those courses rejuvenated my hopes of an athletic career. What could go wrong? Other than all five classes resulting in injuries?

Which they did.

First, tennis resulted in skinned and battered knees that left me lame for most of spring term.

I should have taken the class fall quarter.

Why? Any native knows spring is a perilous time for outdoor sports in northern Minnesota. The air temperatures may lull you into idiocy by rising to a balmy 34° F, but asphalt tennis courts can quickly snap you back to reality by deviously remaining frozen and icy until about…oh… August. Icy and vicious, attacking bare epidermis with all the ferocity of a carnally aroused beaver.

The inner voice re-emerged, challenging, "Enough?"

"Not yet," I replied. "To teach, I have to do this. There are lots more choices. Let me try something else. Something indoors."

So I tried volleyball, which for weeks was warm, fun,

and engaging. In addition to old skills like running and jumping, I learned fun, new ones—bumping, setting, spiking. Defying what PHIL advised, I played hard, polishing my abilities, and enjoying the game until one idiotic play when I jammed four fingers on one hand.

My writing hand.

Nobody ever told me, "Never set a spike."

As I struggled to take notes in my academic classes with those digits taped together, I muttered to myself, "Only three PE credits left."

The inner voice warned, "It can get worse, you know."

Undeterred, I signed up for iceskating. The teacher began the first class by illustrating "the most necessary beginner skill—falling. Not breaking your descent with outstretched arms, but by landing on the body's most effective shock absorber, the 'bottomus maximus' (buttocks)." Before venturing to center ice, she warned, we must demonstrate our ability to "pound ice" painlessly. Only then were we permitted to skate forward, try leg-over-leg turns, practice stops, or attempt to skate backward. Fooling even myself, I easily mastered the art and advanced through all of the basic skills with amazing dexterity.

Except the dreaded T-stops.

There are many ways to stop on skates and I quickly mastered the easiest and the hardest. I could snowplow and run gently into the boards. I could swiftly twist my feet into a hockey stop. But when it came to forming a T with my skates and leaning on the back skate, I always ended on my butt.

Then I noticed this girl who was really good at T-stops on both legs, but could not do a hockey stop. Her ankles didn't work that way.

Hm. A maiden in distress, I thought.

Plus, she was gorgeous.

"Careful," a voice warned.

I ignored it.

Being the eternal champion of amorous opportunities and an all-around good guy, I slid up to her and suggested we help each other with our skating "deficiencies."

Her weak smile should have raised an alarm, but once we started working, the arrangement was perfect. For awhile.

Until it was my turn to illustrate my hockey-stop prowess.

All my confidence and skill deserted me when I needed it most. Not only did I fail to stop, I failed the teacher's most crucial skill—I forgot how to fall butt first, cracking my skull, losing consciousness, and never seeing that class or the girl again.

"Told you," the voice gloated.

Conceding defeat and becoming a night watchman at K-Mart looked tempting, but with graduation only two quarters away, I only needed two more credits.

"Just pick safer sports," I decided. "How about swimming?"

Of course! Swimming! Sure, there was the danger of drowning, but that's why God invented lifeguards.

"It's not an easy *A*," PHIL warned me. "You're kind of a wimp."

"So? Whoever heard of swimming injuries?"

I certainly hadn't—until I took a belly flop off the one-meter board the last day of class and suffered massive bruises to the face, chest, and legs.

One giant mass of pain and purple, I limped through the campus tunnels with a baseball cap pulled low over my face for days to avoid embarrassment. Regardless of the agony, I still managed a smile.

Only one more PE credit left. Success loomed.

Take that PHIL!

In the student union, I grabbed a Coke and a seat to examine my next quarter's class schedule. Between grimaces and groans came the realization, *I've got this! Ballroom dance. Safest for last. How could anybody… Really! Nobody gets hurt in ballroom dance.*

"Except you," PHIL tried to tell me. Stupid voice just wouldn't leave me alone.

Ignoring the admonition, I called my girlfriend and recruited her to take the class with me. "Just think. We can learn all these steps and use them at Spring Formal while everybody else is just gyrating or groping. It will be fun," I said.

She believed me. Silly woman.

After safely completing the class work, we dressed up, had a great meal downtown, and made our way to Beaux Arts Ballroom for the formal. When the dance began, we were in trouble. Unlike the big band music we anticipated, the soft rock songs forced us to adapt the steps we knew to the unfamiliar rhythms. Just as we decided to rest our faux-fox-trot-weary feet in frustration, the band abruptly bounced into "The Beer Barrel Polka," our favorite dance from class. Leaping onto the floor, we laughed and swung our way around the ballroom while ignoring the pointing rockers and gropers who held back with the wallflowers.

In our zeal, we forgot—Well, I forgot—she wore a long dress. A dress I stepped on. A dress that flew over her head as she careened across the floor. A dress that provided no cushion as, unable to catch myself, I landed on top of her.

To add insult to the injury of two jammed wrists (mine), the band stopped playing, turned a light on us, and asked loudly, "Are you two having fun out there?"

We were the only two who didn't laugh.

"The good news," PHIL reminded me that night, "PE is over. Now you can do something else."

That's right! I thought. *As I'm teaching, I can find the right sport. Something more adult, less dangerous. Something like golf or bowling.*

That was not what PHIL wanted to hear. "No. No. I didn't mean a different game. I meant try something more cerebral. Are you listening?"

I wasn't. Who needed to? Certainly not the next Jack Nicklaus or Earl Anthony.

In my initial endeavors at both sports, feats of brilliance encouraged me, feats like amazing chips or putts in golf and a league-high game and series in bowling. I may not have been the best, but I was far from the worst. And I was getting better.

However, proficiency is not always a good thing. As if to prove PHIL's point, competence also brought pain.

Like when a mighty three-iron fairway swing hit a buried rock and sprained a wrist.

Like when a badly-thrown 16-pound bowling ball bounced off my ankle.

It wasn't until the thumb on my throwing hand stuck in a finger hole and swelled to the size of a cucumber—TWICE —that I finally told PHIL, "Okay. I get it. I'm not going to be an athlete. Maybe just a hiker or something."

To which the voice replied, "About that walking thing, maybe you should… Never mind. We'll talk later."

Although those words sounded ominous, I also heard a suggestion of hope, that all the trials and suffering would somehow work out for the best. Later in life when I read Anne Lamott's words, I remembered my youthful athletic ambitions and realized that even in failure, hope exists for a reason: to keep us moving forward—ever forward—even if that means recognizing our limitations, working for something we never suspected we wanted, and leaving behind something we loved.

Whatever the ambition, we must never give up.

But, if we're smart, maybe next time we will try something less painful.

Michael Frickstad

Hopeless Humor or Feathered Funny

"HOPE IS THE THING with feathers that perches in the soul - and sings the tunes without the words - and never stops at all."
   Emily Dickinson

One of the most difficult jobs of a competitive speech coach is helping a student select the proper category in which to perform. At the time I was coaching, Minnesota speech had thirteen categories spread across the broad areas of oral interpretation and public address. This allowed students to capitalize on their strongest abilities—expounding on current events, interpreting existing literature, composition and presentation, group problem solving, or spontaneous thinking.

Unfortunately, now as then, newbies—those with no knowledge of the activity or self-awareness of their own abilities—often come to their first coaching session with only one goal in mind and excited to announce what it is. Clutching their category list/description sheet in their sweaty hands, they nervously sit down across from the coach, awaiting the inevitable question: "Have you thought about which category you want to do?"

Proudly, they sit straight, bob their head, and proclaim,

"Yeah. I want to be funny. Humorous interpretation."

Unabashed by the thud of the coach's skull against the desktop, their faces beam brilliantly.

It's not that coaches don't like to laugh; it's just that the most trite and discouraging words he or she hears every year are "I want to be funny." Far too often, the most accomplished, most gregarious, most creative, most articulate students in the classroom turn into stumbling, stammering, monotone blobs once they stand in front of a classroom with a script in their hands. Without fail, despite those students' greatest intentions, the presentation skills they actually possess could distort Abbot and Costello's "Who's on First?" into Einstein's *Theory of Relativity* as explained by a three-toed sloth speaking Swahili.

No matter how often the coach explains the competitive disadvantages of the category—the difficulty of finding material, the challenges of delivery, and the sheer number of competitors—the student will remain adamant that, despite all the barriers, their comedic skills will somehow just automatically shine through. Even when the reality of competition begins, no matter how many times they finish last in their round, no matter how many times their speech is greeted by glassy-eyed stares, no matter how many judges advise that they concentrate on something more useful like creative auto repair, they cannot be dissuaded. In a monster death grip, they cling to humorous interpretation because they "want to be funny."

Over my 35 years of coaching, who was my most hopeless humorist? That's easy. Liam.

Later revealed as PHIL.

I have to admit when he showed up at my door as an eighth-grader, I was excited. A boy on the speech team? Yes! He could do whatever category he wanted.

Plus, he was going to be great. He was smart. He was fun to be around. Other kids liked him. His very presence would attract new members to the team, both boys and girls.

And yes, he could do humorous. He was actually,

certifiably funny.

At least, in the classroom.

Or in the hall.

Or on the bus.

Or, as it turned out, anywhere but at a speech contest.

That first season Liam tried several different scripts, but the results were always the same. In a round of six students, he'd rank number five. In a round of five, he'd rank five. In a round of four, he'd rank five.

Nobody knew how he did that. Liam thought the judge was hungover from the night before.

Still, that whole first year, he was always cheerful, laughing off his defeats, continuing to work week after week to improve.

He never did.

I was certain that the length of his speech career would be "one and done," so his name on the next-year's sign-up sheet surprised me, that his experience had not dissuaded him. "Welcome back," I told him. "So what do you want to try this year?"

He smiled widely. "I want to be funny. Humorous."

We both laughed.

"No. Seriously," I said.

"I am serious," he assured me. "Everybody says I have a good sense of humor. I can do this. I'm going to keep working at it until I do it right."

I loved his passion, so I relented.

I wish that I could say his presentations improved that freshman year, but they did not. That didn't stop him. Week after week, he lost, and week after week, he came back for more. On every bus ride home, he and his friends laughed off his scores. No matter the results, he planned and practiced, rehearsing every nuance he could think of. Then, at the next tournament, he forgot everything and lost again. "It's okay, he would explain. "I made a bunch of new friends today."

His ability to make friends proved more valuable than his speaking skills. As I had hoped during his initial season, his attitude and perseverance attracted more and more team members. Without winning a single round, he became the student leader the team needed as it grew from an obscure after-school interest into a solid, more prominent, area-recognized squad.

Liam's sophomore year was more of the same, but did show a shift in goals. Still wanting to "be funny," he stuck with humorous interpretation, but rather than shooting for the contest win, he adopted more realistic goals. Like avoiding the rank of five in a round, the worst possible score a judge could give. Instead of getting caught up in rivalry and strife, he, his friends, and his teammates laughingly sported "No 5s" buttons at every meet.

To a certain point, his shift succeeded. Halfway through the season, he received his first 4 in a round of six contestants. When he heard the news on the bus ride home, he bellowed, "I got this!" Focused and re-energized, he eagerly pushed through the rest of the schedule, a schedule in which he never saw anything better than five again.

At the recruitment meeting for his junior year, Liam once again announced his resolution to "be funny."

"You really don't want to try any other category? You might do better," I suggested.

Like every other season, he laughed and shook his head. "I'm a humorous guy, Mr. F. I'm gonna do this."

And the 5s just kept coming. With the addition of an occasional 4 and once even a 3.

Still, his friends began to feel sorry for him. As Liam boarded the bus after a particularly brutal tournament, a girl asked him, "Why do you keep doing this? You never win anything."

He shrugged and said, "I'm having fun. I'll get it someday."

By now, I was scrambling to find someway for Liam to succeed. He was a good kid. He was one of the hardest workers I had ever seen. He deserved something better, something to give him hope, something not only to get him through his junior year, but also to inspire him to finish his high school career on a high note the following season. Even if it was only something that would help him win one round at one tournament.

Nothing worked. His junior year ended as dismally as every other. Any hope of him even showing up for his senior season seemed impossible.

Yet when the recruitment meeting came around, there he was, smiling and excited.

"Humorous?" I asked.

"Yep."

"I want to be funny," we said together.

It would be harder this year. In addition to our regular season of tournaments, our team had joined the National Forensic League, making this an especially significant year for our program. Besides our normal competition, the League membership added another level where winners would advance to a national tournament. But to participate at the qualifier, students had to achieve membership in the League and be selected by their coach. We coaches gave the team this information as an incentive to give their best during the season ahead. We would announce our participants halfway through the season.

I really hoped the incentive would give Liam the boost he needed to finally win something.

He accepted the incentive. He just didn't win. He barely achieved League membership the week before the qualifier.

Barely or not, he was a member, and there was room in our allotment for one more humorous interpreter. The decision to include Liam was simple. For five years, he had worked diligently despite the hardships. Facing defeat every week, he had never given up. Even through seasons of all 5s, he had earned his membership in the NFL. He deserved the honor of participating in our team's initial qualifier, no matter how poorly he did.

Even though the thought of him winning and advancing to nationals was futile.

As a team, all our speakers were realistic. This was a giant step competitively. Nobody expected to win. The goal of the three-day qualifier, the longest single tournament in our history, was to advance to the finals on Saturday. That, in itself, would be a miracle, but logistically we prepared just in case. If there were any finalists, they would compete at the NFL's college site, while those who did not advance would compete at a regular invitational tournament held at a high school in the same town.

Our precautions proved beneficial. Friday night, we learned three of our speakers had broken to finals.

Liam was not one of them. Once more, he had received all 5s during the preliminary rounds.

This time, however, something was different. This time he was not simply accepting of his loss; he was excited. As we exited the bus at home, he rushed to me with his hands waving and with a giant grin.

"Mr. F! Mr. F!"

"Liam, I'm sorry you didn't advance. Just go to the tournament tomorrow and have fun."

"Oh, I'm going to. That's what I wanted to tell you. I figured it out!"

"It? What it?"

"You always told us to have fun, and I have, but this week—NFLs—that's what I needed. Thanks for letting me come. I've got this all figured out now. I can hardly wait for tomorrow."

"Just so you know, it's a big tournament, one of the biggest in the state, but—"

"Have fun. I know. I'm going to!" he exclaimed as he jumped down the steps and raced to his car.

The next morning, most of our team went to the high school while the NFL finalists and I went to the college for the last day of competition. None of our finalists advanced to nationals that Saturday, but they were still proud to have competed with the best in our district. They had exceeded all expectations, and were all thrilled as we drove across town, hoping to arrive at the high school in time for the awards presentation at the invitational. The four of us slipped into the auditorium and found our team as the results were being read.

Finding myself behind Liam, I leaned over and tapped his shoulder.

"How did you do?" I whispered.

"Really good. I had fun. Humorous is next."

I could feel his smile as he turned to the stage, leaned forward, and listened intently.

First, the ribbon winners—those who had done well but not placed in the top six—were called. Two of our team received ribbons, one red and one blue.

Liam still leaned forward, his face pushed into his fists. *Why is he still listening?* I thought. *This isn't like him. Just accept —*

"Will the following medalists in humorous interpretation come to the stage?" the announcer asked.

I sat back, disappointed for Liam.

I shouldn't have been.

Suddenly, our entire team was on its feet. They had heard Liam's name.

"What? Liam? A medalist?" I begged through the screaming and clapping.

"Liam! Liam!" people chanted as Liam floated down the aisle toward the stage. Not only was it our team cheering. It was all those around us. The people who had competed against him all those years of 5s. All the people he had encouraged and befriended.

The cheering intensified as each medalist was announced. The room exploded when the announcer hung the championship medal around Liam's neck. The whole area knew the story of the boy who had lost every round of his career. The boy who worked and hoped and worked and hoped and now—he had won.

When he ran back to the hugs of his ecstatic friends and coaches, he laughed and bounced. "I figured it out. I figure it out," he repeated to them all.

"What did you do?"

"What I always wanted to do."

"Which was what?"

"I was funny!"

Through Liam's example and the words of poets, PHIL taught me the curious thing about hope: Nothing and nobody is hopeless. No matter who and no matter when.

When Emily Dickinson entered Mount Holyoke Female Seminary, the director of students assessed each student's religious faith one of three ways: "established Christian," those who "expressed hope," and those who were "without hope." Ironically, that director labeled Emily as the latter.

Why ironically? Because despite what others thought of her personality, faith and poetry, through years of failure, she learned and persisted; through years of rejection, she experimented and came back for more; through every trial she experienced, she wrote.

Writing was who she was.

She wrote many things nobody ever read when she was alive, but words that would inspire others centuries beyond her lifetime. Words of life and death, joy and sorrow.

And words of hope. Hope and PHIL:

Hope is the thing with feathers

That perches in the soul -

And sings the tunes without the words -

And never stops at all.

In the times we are discouraged and frightened, our hope may be as fragile as Emily's feathered bird, yet it can weather every storm, every trial, every defeat. It never asks a thing, but it gives everything.

Emily Dickinson knew that.

So did Liam.

So should we all.

What Are You Doing Here?

"HOPE LIES IN DREAMS, in imagination, and in the courage of those who dare to make dreams into reality."
Jonas Salk

Routine is comfortable. Routine is reassuring.

Routine is debilitating.

By the time I had reached my forties, I had lived most of my life in a rural setting. Small town. Small school.

Even though I had dreams—some would call delusions —of grandeur and achievement, even though I had enjoyed my time at college in the Minneapolis-St. Paul metro, even though social opportunities had been restricted ever since I returned, there was something safe and familiar that kept me fastened to the rural life I had grown up with.

And then one morning teaching my English 12 class…

One of the most inspiring aspects of teaching high school kids is watching their hopes develop and mature. One of the most frustrating aspects is seeing them restrict their opportunities to achieve those aspirations.

Two senior girls walked into class that morning in a foul mood.

"I hate this town so bad," griped Maddie, the thin, usually-sunny brunette.

"Me too," agreed Lois, her blonde best friend. "I can hardly wait to get out of here to somewhere with something to do."

"Thank God we only have three months and we're out of here."

I looked up from my stack of essays as they walked by. "Where are you going," I asked.

"School," Lois replied.

"I gathered that," I replied, smiling. "Where?"

"Fargo," she answered.

My eyes widened. These were two people I had expected to venture someplace farther away, someplace more exotic, someplace with more opportunities. "Fargo? Why?"

"It's a big town."

I pounded my head with both palms.

"What's wrong?"

"Fargo's your idea of a big town?"

"What's wrong with Fargo?" Cain, a heavyweight wrestler, asked from across the room.

"Nothing. Absolutely not a thing. It's just not really that big."

"Bigger than this place," his buddy Aaron chimed in. By then the entire room had tuned into the conversation.

"That's true," I admitted. "But if you really want to get away, if you really want opportunities, you should think about someplace like the Twin Cities or out of state or…"

"Fargo's out of state," a voice interrupted. I couldn't tell whose.

"North Dakota, yes, but it's only across the river. It's almost as Norwegian as we are," I replied. "If you want different, think different."

"Like what?"

"Some place with things we don't have here. Things like professional sports, theater, different kinds of music, different stores. Heck! Even different kinds of weather. I mean this is your chance, like you say, to get out and discover something you never knew existed."

Maddie, who had innocently started the conversation, nodded, then raised her hand.

"Yes?"

She glanced at Lois, lowered her hand, and said, "Don't take this wrong, but—sports, theater, music—those are things you like. Right?"

"Yeah," I admitted. "A lot."

The two girls glimpsed at each other. Lois picked up the thread. "We were just wondering. What are *you* doing here?"

All eyes in the room trained on me, waiting for an answer. There was no judgment, just earnest curiosity.

No answer came to mind. A quick evaluation revealed an uncomfortable truth: There was really nothing—no romantic connection, no entertainment beyond television and the occasional movie, few cultural opportunities. What *was* I doing there? There was only one answer.

"I don't know."

That answer haunted me all day. I had been stuck in the same place doing the same things for over twenty years. What did I want to do with my life? What was holding me back?

I didn't like the sound of my questions. Especially about being held back. Nothing was bad about a small town. If asked how I felt about life, I would answer "Content," but was content enough? Wasn't there something better somewhere else? What did I hope for?

Hope.

That word stopped me. What is *hope* anyway?

After the room emptied, I grabbed a dictionary which defined the word as "the feeling that what is wanted can be had."

Which meant that to hope, I had to want something.

What did I want?

For the moment I thought in generalities: Something

physical. Something spiritual. An action, an achievement, a feeling. Maybe a reversal of fortune. Something that isn't now, but could be—

No. SHOULD be.

MUST be.

This wasn't helping.

Something. Something. Something.

Be specific.

Like what? What did I hope for?

A new profession? No, that wasn't it. I loved teaching. I loved coaching speech and directing plays. Could I do them somewhere else? In or close to the metro?

Sure, I could.

I wonder…

I began my search for schools, reminding myself that a move was not imperative. I already had tenure where I was. I had seniority in my department. I didn't *have* to go anywhere. I could be selective. Somewhere within an hour of the Twin Cities, especially downtown Minneapolis and its theaters, sports, and orchestra.

Armed with a state highway map and a compass, I drew a circle and began my search. Were there any jobs out there where I'd feel comfortable?

With a quick check of state vacancies, I found there were many. City. Suburbs. Exurbs. Nearby towns.

The list was long and included schools I had been to and loved, schools I had been to and hated, and schools that I didn't even know existed.

Then, to narrow my choices, I divided my interests into three groups: Group A (my top ten, my *definitely try*), followed by twelve I called Group B (my *maybes*), and to be safe, another ten logically named Group C (the *I've-never-heard-of-this-but-it's-within-the-circle-so…* group).

With a game plan in mind, I secretly contacted Bemidji State and gathered my credentials. Nobody had to know. It could just turn out to be an exercise, and that would be fine.

When my transcript arrived, I decided to make the

process real. I gathered my references, wrote my application letters, and addressed the envelopes. Faced by the yawning *LETTERS* slot at the post office, I took a deep breath and slipped the ten Group A envelopes inside. It was happening.

Except it wasn't. I heard nothing. Oh, a few *thank-you-for-your-interest-we'll-let-you-know* letters, but nothing else.

I could have stopped then, but if I was going give this a fair shot, I had to keep at it. Which meant on to Group B.

The results there were even more disheartening. Among the *thank-you* letters, I now received a sprinkling of outright rejections, the *we-regret-to-inform-you-the-position-has-been-filled* letters. The only good news was I still had not received any acknowledgement from several of my top choices. Frustrated, I began to re-evaluate the search.

I get it, I thought. *I'm older. More expensive to hire. Of course, it's hard to get a nibble.*

A more ominous thought struck me. Did I actually want to move? Was the hope of new opportunities really worth the effort?

Lois's question resounded in my brain. "What are you doing here?"

Another voice asked, "What are you hoping for?"

As I thought, I tapped the final ten bound envelopes—Group C—on the post office wall, remembering all the searching and planning I had done. Did I have the guts to go through with this?

What the heck? I thought. I removed the rubber band, slid the envelopes into the slot, and returned to the job I had.

Within a few days, I got a phone call. Not a form letter. A real phone call. One of the group C schools asked me to come for an interview. Could I be there on Friday?

"Uh... I don't kn—I mean. Yes. Certainly. Friday. What time? Where?"

After scheduling the particulars, I called my superintendent and in a jittery voice told her of the appointment. She didn't try to talk me out of the idea as I had expected, as I secretly wished she would. "Good," she said.

"You deserve this. Go for it."

Now I had no excuse.

I went to the interview, not knowing what to expect. Certainly not a three-hour session followed by an introduction to selected English staff and other administrators including the superintendent of schools. The experience felt really good, but...

"Was this good?" I wondered as I drove the four hours home. "How can I know?"

I got my answer the next Monday when the principal who had interviewed me called. "We want you. Here's what we can offer..."

Even before I had scheduled the interview, I had figured a job offer would mean a drop in wages because of the transition. However, the offer I received was nearly the same as I was making at the time. The principal further informed me that given difference between my current salary schedule and theirs, I would make up the difference in very little time. In a year or two at the most.

The offer was too good to turn down. I took a deep breath and said yes.

I was on my way.

I called my superintendent and asked her to keep my decision private until I had signed the contract and everything was set. She agreed and the next day I drove back to my new school to make the move official.

At the principal's office, my hands trembled as I prepared to sign the contract. I hadn't taken the time to be frightened before.

There was much to scare me—a daily schedule with far longer classes, a vastly larger building, a more racially and economically diverse student body. In addition, I had no activities to direct. Speech may come later, the principal said, but right then it was more important to concentrate on teaching and getting to know the students and staff. Even with a drastically more challenging assignment, the future excited me.

I had so much to hope for. Hope for my teaching. Hope for a new community. Hope for new relationships.

After shaking hands with my new boss, I folded my copy of the contract and returned home to begin the transition. I had plans to make.

When I walked into my apartment, the red light on my answering machine blinked auspiciously. "You have four messages," the tape said.

Four messages? About what?

I switched the machine to *Play*.

All four messages came from schools asking to schedule an interview.

All four from Group A.

My first thought was, "Wait! No! I just... Could I... I wanted..."

Then I began to laugh. And laugh. And laugh.

There was no turning back.

Lois's words—later known as PHIL's words—*What are you doing here?* may have sparked my imagination, but the images they inspired quickly became hope, and with that hope came the courage to make them a reality.

Reality was now and ahead of me, not what could have been.

The superintendent in her best PHIL impression assured me I deserved this. It was time to go for it.

Bountiful Blossoms

"LORD SAVE US ALL from old age and broken health and a hope tree that has lost the faculty of putting out blossoms."
Mark Twain

The golfing was finished for the annual faculty best-ball tournament—a night of fun to celebrate the end of the school year. No pressure. Just good times with colleagues, fresh air, relaxation. The after party had just started, but I was done for the day. I was tired.

I wasn't usually tired. Yes, I was getting older, but late 50s is not old, not old enough to be exhausted after a couple hours riding around on a golf cart.

"I think I need to go home," I told my friend Ricki.

"You okay?" she asked.

"Yeah. Nothing a couple of Tylenol won't cure."

I could tell by her cocked head and squinty eyes when she dropped me off she wan't convinced. She said, "Call me in the morning and let me know how you're doing. You have my number."

She knew me too well.

"On speed dial. Talk to you then."

I let myself into the house and walked downstairs into the television room. I emptied my change, keys, and flip phone onto a tray table, skipping my usual routine of decompression by watching television before bed. After taking time to brush my teeth and take my blood pressure pill, I headed down the hall to the bedroom and wrapped myself in the covers. I was asleep in seconds.

About 6:00 a.m., I awoke to use the bathroom. I was still groggy, but definitely better than when I went to sleep. *A little longer and I'll be fine*, I thought.

Except I wasn't.

After about an hour more of sleep, my eyes blinked open.

This isn't right, I thought.

I couldn't tell why, so I closed my eyes and turned onto my back. Slowly, cautiously, I opened my eyes again.

The ceiling, the light fixture, the entire room spun wildly. I clutched at the mattress and shut my eyes.

Definitely not right.

With a firm grip on the sheets and blanket, I cracked my eyes open again. The room still spun.

I need help, but how?

I couldn't use the phone. The landline at my bedside hadn't worked for months and my cell phone was down the hall. How would I get there? Walking through a whirling room was for acrobats, not klutzes like me.

"About that walking thing…"

I remembered those words, but not who said them.

It doesn't matter. Maybe I can crawl.

I opened my eyes again, then snapped them shut. The whirling hadn't slowed.

This is bad. This is really bad. What is going on?

"You know. You're thinking. That's good. It's going to be difficult, but you can do this."

What if this is a stroke? I don't know if I can crawl either. I have to do something. I have to get that cell phone.

"Yes. First step."

With my eyes clenched and my hands wrapped around the sheets, I decided, difficult or not, I would sink gently to the floor—ease out from under the covers and slowly lower my legs and body—then roll, slide, squirm and whatever I could to get to that cell phone.

I crashed to the floor.

Everything hurt. My head, my chest, my arms. Facedown, I groaned into the carpet. I could barely breathe, but I could lift my head.

That's a good sign, isn't it?

My eyes clamped shut, I tried to rise to my hands and knees, but dropped back to the floor.

"Nope," I gasped. "But I need to get to that phone."

"Yes, you do. Keep your head down. Push with your legs. Pull with your arms. No giving up."

Gathering all the strength I could, I managed to pull myself inch by inch toward the open door. I prayed aloud, "Lord, get me to the phone and help me call Ricki. She can help me."

Every two lunges forward, I repeated the words. "Lord, get me to the phone and help me call Ricki. She can help me."

With every plea came the assurance, "I hear you."

Through the door, down the hall, into the television room, I pulled and prayed.

When I finally saw the tray table, I rejoiced, but I also realized I had another problem. I was flat on my stomach. How was I going to get the phone?

It didn't matter. I kept advancing and repeating the prayer. "Lord, get me to the phone and help me call Ricki. She can help me."

"I hear you."

At the side of the table, I collapsed, breathing heavily.

"It's okay. You're here. Rest and regroup. Rest and regroup."

Resting proved impossible. I had to get that phone off the tray. What was I going to do? With my face flat on the carpet next to the tray table legs, I recognized my right side was basically worthless. I had crawled all the way from my room by pulling myself with my left hand even though I was right-handed.

Great. But now how could I climb up a TV tray?

Then I had a brilliant idea. I didn't have to climb anything. Obviously, I still had one good hand. I could simply tip the table and let the phone land on the carpet. It wouldn't roll too far. All I needed to do was flip it open and hit Ricki's speed dial number.

But how was I going to do that? My left hand was beneath me. I would have to turn over. I didn't know if I could—

"Reach for it," a voice said.

Okay. This isn't some Hallmark movie—

"Reach for it.

"Reach for—?" I mumbled aloud.

"The phone. Reach for it."

"But I can't—"

No more words came. Somehow, my worthless right hand raised, flung itself upward, bounced off the top of the table, and landed next to my face. In it was my flip phone, open and ready to dial.

"Help me," I prayed.

"I hear you."

A finger punched Ricki's number.

After several rings, her whispered voice answered. "Mike? Why are you calling me so early? You know I've got band practice—"

"I need help," I groaned.

"What?"

"I need help."

"I don't understand. What are you saying?"

Once again, I tried.

"You—Are you— No. Never mind. You need help, don't you?"

Isn't that what I said?

"I'm going to call the EMTs. You stay close to the phone and I'll call you back. Okay?"

"Okay," I replied.

At least, that's what it sounded like to me.

The phone went dead. I lay on the floor, my eyes shut tight, waiting.

"When the phone rings, help me answer," I prayed.

"I hear you."

When it did, a self-prompted finger activated it.

"Mike! Mike, are you there?" Ricki called.

"Yes," I mumbled.

"The EMTs are on their way. I'm going to stay on the line until they get there. Let me talk to them when they do."

"Okay," I said.

"Hey, I understood you. I didn't when you first called. That's good. Just hang on."

"I'm hanging."

In the distance, I heard a siren. "They're coming," I said.

"I hear them. Let me know when they're inside."

There was a pounding on the front door.

"Mr. Frickstad! Mr. Frickstad! Are you in there?"

"I'm here," I called. I doubted they could hear me.

A crash shattered the door jamb. Heavy feet stomped up the stairs above me. Noise. Confusion. Voices shouting.

"Mr. Frickstad! Mr. Frickstad! What's his first name?"

"Mike."

"Mike! Where are you?"

"I'm down here," I called as loudly as I could.

Nobody heard. One set of footsteps rumbled across the floor above while another clambered down the steps.

"Found him! Found him!"

In seconds two men huddled around me, one checking my eyes, my arms, my speech, while the other spoke to Ricki.

With his face close to mine, the larger one told me, "Okay. We think you've had a stroke, but we won't know for sure until we get you to a hospital. All right?"

"That's what I thought."

"Where do you usually go?"

"Buffalo or Elk River."

"They're pretty small. They can't help you. We're going to take you to Mercy. Okay? They have a stroke facility."

"I don't care. I'm broken. Fix me."

"We'll do our best."

Things got worse before they got better.

I spent three weeks in the hospital where doctors found that, in fact, I had had two strokes in two different parts of the brain—one a block, one a bleed. Just how much damage had been done was going to take awhile to assess. Even though I could speak, I could not walk. Even though I could move my limbs roughly, much of my right side was still paralyzed. Even though I could see, I could not focus my eyes together. I was plagued with double vision unless one eye was closed. While checking out my brain, doctors also found a hole in my heart.

Treatment was going to be tricky, they told me. Recovery would be long and arduous.

"Will I ever be the same?" I asked my neurologist and cardiologist.

They were bluntly honest. "Probably not, but you will improve. Life will be harder, but still worth living."

"What does that mean?"

"Hang on. Keep working. You'll see."

"Keep hoping?"

"Exactly."

Hope came in drips and drabs. Officials found me a spot at Sister Kenny Institute, a rehab hospital known for its work with stroke patients. Work in that gym got me on my feet. Before long, I was using a walker, then a cane, and eventually balancing on my own feet. Acupuncture helped me relax. Water therapy gave me strength and confidence. Music therapy reminded me of the joy of song.

Although that hope was good in the moment, it was temporary. Hope for the future was difficult to find. My hand —my right hand—the hand I used to write, to brush my teeth, to cut my food, to play my guitar—had little strength or dexterity. Even if I could walk unaided again, without the use of that right hand, I couldn't see how life was going to improve.

One morning, my occupational therapist Luke came into my room with an ominous grin on his face which could only mean one thing: He had a new goal in mind for me.

Sister Kenny liked goals.

As a teacher, I too appreciated the practice. Goals give learning direction, a destination to reach for. So far in rehab, they had worked well.

On the bad side, new goals also mean more work. At Sister Kenny, the therapists' goals were not always the ones I wanted to meet. Even if they were good for me.

"What's up today?" I asked.

"You are going to put on your own shoes," Luke answered.

"Ooh. Wow," I scoffed.

"I know it doesn't sound like that big a deal, but can you do it?"

I thought a moment. "Well, not yet."

"Ready to give it a try?"

"Sure."

Luke handed me my high-top tennis shoes.

What was I thinking? I had trouble putting these on when I was normal.

Setting the right one aside, I held the left one in both hands, planning my method of attack. I loosened the laces, stretched the top open, then looked up for approval.

"Good," he said. "Ready to try it on?"

I took a deep breath, bent over, and slipped my foot inside. I held onto the tongue and back as I pushed my heel down until it thumped into place. With my foot securely covered, I pulled the laces tight.

"I think it worked," I said proudly.

"I think you're right. Here's the second one," he said, handing me the mate.

I groaned and repeated the process. It was easier the second time and with little effort, I stood up at the side of the bed with both feet in my shoes.

"Good job," he said. "Wow. I thought you'd have more trouble. I didn't plan on doing anything else this morning"

I laughed. "I suppose now you're going to tell me to tie them."

He laughed with me, then suddenly turned serious. "Well, I wasn't going to, but since you suggested it, do you want to try?"

"I don't—uh—"

I had backed myself into a corner. What if I failed? Would I ever try again? Would I have to have somebody tie my shoes forever? Worse yet, would I be stuck in a world of velcro forever?

I looked at Luke.

"I think you can," he encouraged.

I took a deep breath, bent over the left shoe and grabbed a lace end in each hand.

I can remember this, I decided.

Carefully, I intertwined the ends and pulled the laces snug.

"Good. Remember, you don't have to do it all in one breath."

I laughed and inhaled, exhaled, once, twice. "I can do this. I can do this," I repeated to myself.

Even with my stiff, clumsy right fingers, I formed a loop. My tongue pushed between my lips as I wrapped the other end around the loop and pushed the lace through to form the second loop.

I'm doing this.

I pinched both loops and pulled them tight. "I think I—"

I glanced up for confirmation.

"You did it."

I felt pressure behind my eyes.

"I did it."

I sat back.

"You want me to do the second one?" he asked, reaching for my right foot.

"No! No. I want to."

He sat back. "Go for it."

I reached forward. "Intertwine…loop…loop…pull."

I sat back.

"You did them both!"

Tears flooded my face. "I did them both."

He opened his arms and let me hug him. "This is big," he whispered. "This is really big."

"Yeah," I replied, backing up and wiping the tears from my eyes. "There *is* hope."

He looked deep into my eyes. "There's always hope. Remember that."

I nodded. "There's always hope."

That was all over a decade ago. According to the federal government, I am now officially a senior citizen, and I have to admit I often forget to remember the lesson of that shoe-tying day.

That's what old people do. We forget.

And let's face it: one of the easiest things to forget with old age is hope. However, I've also learned the more I can preserve my memory, the more I can maintain hope as well.

Why?

Because, no matter how traumatic, how agonizing, or persistent my experiences may be, the blessings of life have a way of sticking in my brain and transforming tragedy and sorrow to beauty and joy, strength and thanksgiving.

Of the day of that stroke—a day of agony and terror—I remember the answered prayers that got me to the phone and put it in my weakened hand. I remember Ricki's voice answering the call and finding me help. I remember the EMTs who saved me. I remember the doctors telling me to keep hoping.

Of rehab, I remember the therapists celebrating each victory on my way to recovery, no matter how small. I remember the treks across the gym, first in a walker, then with a cane, and finally on my own two feet. I remember floating in the therapy pool and the water gently lapping on my face and arms. I remember the vibration of a guitar against my stomach.

Through it all I remember the face of my pastor, first at the end of the driveway as the EMTs drove me away, then in the hospital, at Sister Kenny as I struggled to cross the gym floor, and in my living room, telling me it was okay to ask God "Why me," that I wouldn't be human if I didn't.

What I remember most from that experience are two biblical promises from the book of Romans. First, Romans 8:28, one that I had heard, read, and said innumerable times: "And we know that in all things God works for the good of those who love him, who have been called according to his purpose." Second, and the one that has sustained me for years since, Romans 8:38-39: "For I am convinced that neither death nor life, neither angels nor demons, neither the present nor the future, nor any powers, neither height nor depth, nor anything else in all creation, will be able to separate us from the love of God that is in Christ Jesus our Lord."

Old age cannot kill those memories. The voice of PHIL speaks in them all, so that long after those events, I've arrived at the same important conclusion Mark Twain did: There is hope.

A living, growing, eternal tree of hope. That hope tree blooms in me.

Its branches are thick and broad, brimming and bountiful with more than blossoms and leaves. Every day, every month, every year, it provides an abundant harvest of joy, love, laughter, warmth, and intimacy—all the blessings God has always wanted to give.

God and His Angels

"FOR I KNOW THE plans I have for you, declares the Lord, plans for welfare and not for evil, to give you a future and a hope."
Jeremiah 29:11 (ESV)

Too often when life falls to pieces—loss, betrayal, sorrow, emptiness, grief—somebody will say helpfully, "It's all part of God's plan. Just accept it and move on." As well intentioned as those words are, as somebody once told me, "they really suck."

Why?

Because nobody enmeshed in depression and misery is moving anywhere. You're not even getting out of bed.

All you can do is appreciate the concern and ignore the words, remembering God's plan is NOT for evil. God's plan is for welfare and love. Anything else comes from elsewhere. What you need to hear when disaster strikes is that no matter how abandoned you feel, you are not alone. You need to be reminded that God shares your anguish and it's okay to wail and rage at Him. He understands and hurts with you.

The good news is when your heaving chest calms down, when your tears dry, when you can feel the strength of the earth under you feet once more, God will reveal what you really need to hear. One word of caution, though: God doesn't always look or sound like you expect. Make sure you're listening.

I sat at the table alone and apprehensive. I had missed the first evening of the local NAMI (National Alliance on Mental Illness) Family to Family Program and I wasn't even sure I wanted to be there.

"What good is it going to do?" I asked Diane. "It's not going to cure anybody."

"No, but it might make you feel better," she replied.

So hours later, there I sat, still not persuaded, aimlessly flipping through her handouts from the previous week.

I should have been reading, but the pages would not focus. Instead, I saw a garbage bag lying next to the front door, stuffed with clothes, a phone, a toothbrush, and a hairbrush.

I shook off the image and gazed into space.

Despite its beige walls, fluorescent lights, and wide windows allowing in the warm rays of sunset on the mountains, the room felt dark. I squeezed my eyes shut.

The bag disappeared, but the door swung open in the wind.

I shook my head and blinked myself back to reality.

Fellow class members shuffled in. Some averted their eyes, eyes sunken from days and nights of weeping and waiting for answers. Others gathered in protective clumps supported by shattered dreams. Still more discreetly stopped for coffee and cookies, hoping either caffeine or sugar could rejuvenate a trace of their lost lives. Across the empty center of the room, another couple sat at another table, like me, reviewing the course material from the previous week.

They don't look any more comfortable than I feel, I thought.

At the portable whiteboard at the front of the room, Diane chatted with the class facilitator—a short, elderly woman wearing a hand-printed name tag. *Belle,* it said.

The woman's energetic smile and wild gestures intimidated me. I did not need to see happy.

Or even calm.

I turned back to Diane's notebook, dipped my head, shaded my eyes with both hands, and ignored the room.

It's one night. Just one night.

If I'm lucky.

With one hand still at my forehead, I picked up a highlighter with the other as I searched the handouts for any special phrase worth remembering. Never approaching paper, the highlighter spun between my fingers, uncomfortably poised above the binder.

The words did not make sense to me, but not because they were strange or intimidating. I was educated enough to recognize them all, understand their meaning, even believe what they were trying to say to me, but they would not stand still. They danced around the pages, eluding my focus.

I slapped the table, puffing in frustration. Diane slid into the seat next to me and whispered, "You have to let it go for a couple hours."

I covered my face with both hands and pulled my fingers over my cheeks.

The room faded into images of a sick, shivering body huddled in a doorway, the same person lying unconscious in an alley. Like a television voiceover, I heard the words of a police officer—"We regret to inform you…We found…We found…"

I prayed the images and words would never be real, but with every passing day—I shook away the ideas. That's why Diane and I were at NAMI. Perhaps they would teach what was happening to us.

"Shall we get started?" Belle called to the room. Because Diane had raved about the woman the previous week, I had vowed to withhold criticism. However, with each breath of Belle's enthusiasm, I was failing the endeavor.

I covered my fuming scowl with a single hand and glared silently.

After everybody had found their seats and snapped the week's handouts into their three-ring notebooks, class finally began with all the prerequisite introductions and business, but there was definitely a division of labor. While the women actively participated in the openings, the men quietly absorbed and analyzed the class mechanics and the underlying tension of the room.

Tension? Why is that here? We're supposed to be here for help. Where's this strain coming from?

Everybody appeared pleasant and engaged, but I could detect wringing hands barely hidden in laps, clenched jaws, and shifting eyes. The anxiety in the room was real.

Outside, the last sliver of sun dropped behind the mountains.

"We have some new people here tonight. Why don't we go around the room and introduce ourselves? Tell us your name and a brief reason why you're here. Let's start here on my right," Belle said, walking toward Diane and me.

I sighed and looked up to the ceiling.

Testimonies.

I knew they would be part of the evening, but not this soon. I didn't want to talk. I didn't want to think. I wanted to go home.

"Diane?" Belle asked.

"You heard from me last week and Mike's kind of uncomfortable," Diane said taking my hand. "Can somebody else start?"

"Sure," Belle said.

Diane's hand, as well Belle calmly walking past me, relaxed my nerves. I was safe for now.

As each family told their story, I realized I really was safe. Our situation was far less devastating than the others' in the room. No violence. No injuries. No prisons. No hospitals. As lonely and empty as we felt, we had each other, we had our extended family, we had God. We were blessed.

Diane squeezed my hand. I felt a lightness, a glimmer of hope.

Finally, the testimony circuit found its way back to us. Belle stood before me. "Ready?" she asked. "It won't be that bad. I promise."

Belle and our classmates—their faces, their shared tears, and gentle nods—encouraged me.

I gulped, glanced at Diane, and said, "I guess."

"What can we do for you?" Belle asked.

I shrugged.

"I don't know. Nothing, I guess. I'm just so frustrated. I mean I'm a guy. I've been a teacher and a dad. I'm supposed to fix things, but all this has just been too much. I can't fix a thing."

The man sitting next to me, whispered, "It's okay. Tell us. You'll be fine. We'll all be fine."

As much as the fear and anger and frustration tore at me, in those moments I spoke of them, I felt safe and supported. I took a deep breath, sighed, and squeezed Diane's hand.

The remainder of the class, which was made up of lectures and notes, proceeded easily. Diane and I felt no breakthroughs, no "aha" moments, but we knew we were not alone. Everyone in the room shared the same pain, the same tears, the same love for the wounded and afflicted.

As the session ended for the evening, I capped my highlighter and closed our binder. I stood and looked about the room, searching for something or someone. I didn't know what.

"Are you okay?" Diane asked me.

I nodded. "I just wish—I don't know."

I couldn't describe my emotion to anybody, not even my wife. I had to admit I felt better than when I came, but I was still lost. I saw no end to the anxiety, the reflex to fix everything, the hopelessness I had been feeling for weeks.

"You!" Belle cried from across the room. She pointed an accusatory finger at me. "I want to talk to you before you leave!"

Her strident, commanding voice was completely out of character for the woman who had just calmly taught us how to deal with the mentally ill. Tentatively, I handed the class notebook to Diane and wound my way through the exiting crowd to the tiny woman with the powerful voice. Patiently, I waited in line as other students asked her questions. When the last one finished, I glanced behind me to make sure Diane hovered close enough in case I needed her.

She sensed my fear and twisted her way toward me through the crowd.

I licked my lips and stepped forward to Belle.

"You wanted to…"

Before I could finish my sentence, Belle snatched my arm and pulled me aside.

"First of all, thank you for coming tonight and relating your story, but I couldn't let you leave tonight without telling you something."

"What's that?"

"Your life is going to be all right. It really is." She shook my arm. "Do you believe me?"

I glanced back at Diane as she took my other arm protectively.

"I…I guess. I know it's all part of God's plan, but—"

"Oh, bull shit."

Diane's head and mine snapped up.

"I'm sorry," Belle said. "I didn't mean to swear, but God didn't plan for this to happen to you. I don't care what anybody says. Blame somebody else for that. But I can tell you what God IS planning. He's planning to bring something good out of it all."

I bit my lip and turned away. Belle grabbed me and squinted mercilessly into my eyes. "You don't believe me because you can't see how, right?"

I gulped. "Right."

"Honestly? You don't have to, but I'm going to tell you anyhow. All the people you heard about tonight? The parents, the cousins, those afraid to leave the house, even those wandering homeless on the street? Those people are smart. That's how they survive. They figure out what they need to do and they do it. That's how they've gotten where they are."

"I guess," I mumbled to lower the volume as I edged closer to Diane.

Belle would not let me escape. She moved closer. "Listen. I've been through this. There's no guessing. These people know more than we can ever guess, but that's not all. You know who else is smart?"

"Who?"

"You! You and everybody you met here tonight. You're all smart. Like the people you all talked about, you can survive this. You know why?"

"Why?" I whispered.

"Because God is taking care of you. You believe in God, right? You said that, didn't you?"

I first looked at Diane, then back at Belle. "You said this is not God's pla—"

"Forget that. I'm asking do you believe in God?"

I gulped and nodded.

"Really?" Belle demanded.

"Yes. Really," I answered.

She punched my arm and laughed. "I know you do, but I want you to listen to me. I'm not making this up. I've been where you are. People kept feeding me all that—hogwash—Is that a better word?"

I smiled and nodded.

"Okay. Hogwash about God's plan. He didn't plan this junk for any of us. He plans good stuff. We're the ones who mess it up and make it bad, not Him. But you know what's really good about God? I mean really, really good?"

"What?"

"No matter how bad life gets, He *will* bring good out of it."

I shifted my weight, remembering how I had met Diane a year after my stroke. "I understand that, but it's hard to see —"

"I know it is! With all the crap that happens to us, it's easy to forget. That's why I'm reminding you. Listen to me. I've seen hundreds of these people, and every one of them—

every ONE of them!—has a guardian angel watching over them. They shouldn't survive, but they do. Somehow, someway, they find a way. God picks them up and gives them what they need.

"Now here's the most important lesson of the night. Not the science, not the statistics. It's this: You—Michael—you may be a guy, a teacher, a dad, but you can't fix this. You may been good at fixing a lot of things, but this is out of your league. You have to let God and His angels do it. That's the way it works. Not you. God. Can you let Him?"

My chin trembled. "Let go and let God?" I murmured.

Belle smiled. "I know that's a cliché, but yes."

I felt like a second-grader being chewed out by the teacher when he knows she's right. "Okay," I whispered.

"Good. And you'll help him?" she asked Diane.

My wife smiled and nodded.

"Come here and hug me, you two," Belle said, grabbing us both and squeezing us into her tiny arms.

I closed my eyes. *For a future and a hope, God works for good*, I thought. I nodded and hugged Diane closer. *This—THIS—was God's plan*.

In the darkness, the glimmer of hope became a ray of peace, love, and faith.

Integrity

The Notorious Squirt Gun Caper

"FINALLY, BROTHERS AND SISTERS, whatever is true, whatever is noble, whatever is right, whatever is pure, whatever is lovely, whatever is admirable—if anything is excellent or praiseworthy—think about such things."
Philippians 4:8 (NIV)

It was tough being an adolescent rebel in the 1960s, living in a northern Minnesota town of less than 200 people (Tenstrike) and going to a school ten miles away in the urban metropolis that was four times that size (Blackduck).

All right. Maybe *tough* is the wrong word. Actually, *rebel* is probably the least accurate word in that sentence.

To be honest, I was not much of a troublemaker. There was no trouble to make. I was more of a super nerd before I even knew what a nerd was. The extent of my high school insurrection was three-fold: being the first to own a Trapper Keeper notebook, wearing a Beatle-inspired Nehru jacket for class pictures, and adding a male presence to the local Spanish class. My only real brush with infamy came in ninth grade and the notorious squirt-gun caper (NSGC).

I told you I was a nerd.

It was springtime, that time of year when a young man's mind turns to mush and mayhem, which meant trying to impress girls by being a jerk. I had a hard time with the former, but I was great at the latter. I was especially adept at taking good things and turning them into true dorkiness.

The good thing?

Our small school had a unique final testing policy that stated if you had an A average for the year in any class, you were exempt from the final exam for that class. In fact, you could leave the building, hang out at the bakery, take a walk, or just go explore the town. After that fifteen minute exercise, you were forced to use your imagination. Which was a dangerous proposition.

That was the genesis of the NSGC.

I was a pretty successful student that freshman year. The only classes I needed to attend that last week were physical education (I was not an athlete), shop (the teacher hid all the hammers, saws, and screwdrivers when I was in the same wing of the building so I wouldn't hurt myself), and science (too many unpronounceable, multisyllabic words).

My mother told me all year she was proud of me, that Bs in those three classes was good enough for her. Unfortunately, Mom's approval didn't get me out of those finals. Although I would have been a lot more fortunate had I settled for "good enough" in math, English, and civics to keep me in the building and out of trouble.

The morning of the math final, three of us—Barry, Alan, and I—had this really subversive idea that rather than sitting in the cafeteria picking our noses, we would go downtown (two short blocks) and buy squirt guns to raise havoc at lunchtime.

Two things to note about this community: First, it was so small the merchants knew every kid in school, and second, customer confidentiality was not a store policy.

Anywhere.

So, when three dorky freshmen showed up in the local hardware store looking for the "squirt gun department" as they jostled and bragged about their future exploits, it wasn't going to be a well-kept secret. Unbeknownst to us, our plans beat us back to the building.

The first clue that our plan was in jeopardy was the sight of Mr. Zakarias, the scowling principal, waiting outside the main door to the school, his long arms crossed sternly, his short chin tucked into his chest, his squinty eyes glaring over his horn-rimmed glasses. From half a block away, we knew enough to shut up, but not enough to avoid that entrance entirely. Instead, weaving nervously up the sidewalk with false bravado, we kept moving toward the door, our sweaty hands unconsciously covering the weapons hidden in our pockets.

As we approached the entrance, Barry and Alan wisely held back to let me take the heat. I was dumb enough to keep walking. Their willingness to sacrifice me for the common good really didn't affect Mr. Z's strategy. He would have picked me anyway. He knew who the weak link was. He lowered his glasses on his nose, and his stern eyes narrowed to mere slits as I approached, gulping and wiping my trembling hands on my pants.

He didn't move. Not out of the way. Not toward me. He just stood there solid, looming, imposing.

He knows about the squirt guns. I knew it. *But that doesn't make sense. How could he?*

I gulped and wobbled to an awkward stop. I had no idea what to do or say. I glanced back at the other boys, who provided no help at all. They both massaged their necks and looked away in opposite directions. I scratched my head and turned back to Mr. Zakarias, who simply extended one hand toward me.

"Wha—" My voice cracked. "What?" I finally squawked.

His hand didn't move.

I knew exactly what he wanted, but I had just spent—

He wouldn't give up. Why wouldn't he move? His hand remained extended as his eyes bore into my skull.

"Just give it to him," my conscience told me.

Sucking in a slow, shaky breath, I dug into my pocket and brought out the squirt gun.

The sun reflected off the clear blue plastic. It had never been filled. It would have been so fun—girls screaming, boys running, teachers bellowing.

I gazed at the open palm. It was no use.

I handed it to him. My head hung low as I stepped aside and let the others relinquish theirs as well. Sliding all three guns into his suit jacket pocket, Mr. Zakarias turned and opened the door for us.

Still, a question hung in the air.

The other boys weren't going to ask it. Their eyes told me, "It's not our job. You ask him."

I rubbed my arm and stammered, "Will we get those back at the end of the day?"

He held the door silently.

After a furtive glance at each other, we stuffed our hands into our empty pockets, exhaled, and filed into the building, frustrated, guilty, and unarmed.

What does this goofy little story of dorkiness have to do with PHIL?

Integrity.

In his letter to the Philippians, the apostle Paul tells us to think about truth. That's what integrity is—thinking about truth. Not truth the way we want it, but the way it is. Integrity is recognizing undeniable facts and and living with reality. If we had first thought at all, we would have recognized the truth of the great squirt-gun caper: it was a dumb idea.

There was no way it could turn out positive. No matter how selective our attacks would be, we would have squirted the wrong person. Somebody bigger. Somebody willing to hold a grudge forever.

The store clerks and Mr. Zakarias saved us from our own idiocy, the revenge of the soaked, and our parents' anger. However, there was a more long-lasting lesson to the escapade. An example manifested by the principal's impeccable integrity.

He had so many other options on how to handle the situation. He could have stomped and shouted. He could have purposely embarrassed us. He could have whipped out the "board of education" and paddled our butts blue. Worse, he could have called a parental meeting and scarred us for life.

Instead, before we were in sight of the building, he weighed the situation, the repercussions, and potential damage, then decided that what was necessary was not a display of power and authority. Instead, he relied on his strength of character and his faith in our developing morality. By opting for silent yet forceful action, Mr. Z taught us what we needed to know forever: the futility of excuses and lies. He simply cut through the gunk we would use to excuse our conduct and compelled us to follow our inner voices—our voices of PHIL—to make our own decisions, the morally right decisions, the only admirable decisions.

He trusted us to have the integrity of doing the right thing and not being stupid dorks.

Michael Frickstad

The Courage to Say No

"HAVE THE COURAGE TO say no. Have the courage to face the truth. Do the right thing because it is right. These are the magic keys to living your life with integrity."
W. Clement Stone

The courage to say *no*—to others and yourself—can be truly life-shaping no matter your age or circumstances. It's especially important in adolescence when values are formed and tested by curiosity, desire, and peer pressure.

When I was fourteen, I learned the truth of my parents' divorce when I was a toddler, how alcoholism had enslaved my father and demolished his relationship with my mother, even severing his connection with his own parents.

Who told me?

His father.

That was the year my father invited me to come visit him in Colorado for a summer. I hadn't seen him since I was five, so I was excited. My mother, on the other hand, was adamant that I was not going. I was not only disappointed, I was angry. The tension in our house was thick for days until I received an intervention letter from my grandfather, relating stories of the physical and emotional terror my mother endured, how her injuries and fear prompted him to aid her escape, and how alcohol ravaged my father's health, personality, and productivity.

I relented to my mother's wishes. Not only did I decline the visit, I decided I could never let myself become like my father.

That resolution did not come easily. Since I had entered junior high, enticing rumors of drinking parties had circulated the halls, rumors mostly about older students, but there was also the unspoken maxim that the younger you drank, the cooler you were. In the 60s, cool was king.

I wanted to be cool.

However, since my grandfather's letter, I couldn't give people a reason to say "Like father, like son." Cool or not, I had to have the courage to say *no*.

When I first informed friends of my decision, I defensively claimed my resolution was neither religious nor moral, but a personal commitment to protect my mother from memories better left in the past. But, of course, as time went by, life repeatedly confronted me with the ramifications of that choice. I went to parties, but I would only sip what others swallowed. I just could not bring myself to do more. Eventually, even the hint of alcohol grew repugnant.

As it all worked out, courage to say *no* was never really a concern in high school. There weren't that many people to say it to. Cool was never a factor. My close friends understood; all others concluded coercion wasn't worth the effort and allowed me to be who I was.

Then there was college. Where conviction meets reality.

When I moved from a town of 112 hermits to a campus of 60,000 socially-released savages, temptation soared. Add the lure of Minnesota-style psychedelia and hippiedom, coupled with raging hormonal imbalances and agonizing lust, I had things to see and people to do.

I was confused, but I was hundreds of miles away from prying eyes. I didn't care.

Except I did.

Although opportunities to defy "the Establishment" norms flourished, I talked a better rebellious game than I was willing to play.

Even when presented with the chance of a lifetime.

One fall night, some friends from the Whole Coffeehouse invited my roommate/guitar friend Barry and me to a riverside party on the banks of the Mississippi near the Washington Avenue Bridge. "It'll be fun," they said. "And bring your guitars so you can sing all those goofy songs you guys play."

I wasn't sure that's how I wanted to be known, but there would be girls, so…yeah. We went.

Getting there was not an easy task. First, we had to wind our way down the cliff-side stairway carrying our guitar cases. Then we skirted through the dark, spooky parking lot, and searched the lower edge until we found the dirt path along the river. From there, we pushed our way ducking and swearing through the concealing dry brush to a circular opening.

Breaking from the woods, we discovered the campfire. Later than we intended, but we were finally there. Now where were we going to set up? The eclectic crowd had already divided itself into three distinct groups and claimed their own territories.

Farther downstream, Group One—the acidheads— congregated to take substances that, yes, we had heard of, but had never seen or used. That was a totally different game than either of us wanted to play. Not for us, we decided.

A bit closer to the fire and our sensitivities was Group Two, those with one foot in the experimental camp and one in the traditional "let's get smashed" flock, the ones with a joint in one hand and a beer in the other. These people were not as scary, but were still outside our comfort zone.

Lastly, Group Three, by far the largest group, the one where we knew the most people, hung around a keg adding degrees of inebriation by pouring more beer and swigging from unknown bottles hidden in paper sacks.

I didn't feel totally at ease, but standing next to the keg

was my favorite Whole volunteer.

Blonde hair. Long and straight flowing down her back. Dark, arched eyebrows over silver blue eyes. A smile as wide as Montana. A laugh that could tickle a raging penguin.

Patricia.

And her boyfriend.

I often forgot his name, so I just called him Alf. He'd laugh, thinking I was making a joke, comparing him to *Mad* magazine's Alfred E. Neuman. In reality, I didn't know him and really didn't want to.

"This looks promising," I told Barry, nodding toward Patricia.

He rolled his eyes and began unpacking his guitar. I had told him of my infatuation too many times.

We found a vacant log near the fire and began playing the silly songs we were known for. Before long we had attracted an eclectic bunch of revelers—loud, hilarious, and plastered. As much fun as we were having, I maintained a secret eye on Patricia and Alf.

As we sang "Froggy Went A-Courtin'," I noticed the two of them arguing quietly, but vehemently. Patricia leaned into Alf, poked his chest, and said something that made him turn and walk away defiantly toward Group Two.

I averted my eyes, trying not to pay attention, playing louder and making up new verses, which confused Barry.

Laughing, he elbowed me and asked, "What are you playing?"

"I dunno," I answered, my eyes searching the crowd for Patricia. "Just riffing, I guess."

Barry followed my line of sight, then broke off with a grin. "Yeah. Riffing. I get it."

He knew who I was looking for.

I scowled. Maybe one of us could laugh, but I needed to keep eye on both Patricia and Alf, one I liked, the other I wanted to dunk in the river.

After we finished several folk-style protest songs, we segued back to silly with "Sweet Violets," one of our biggest crowd pleasers. After we finished and acknowledged the scattered applause, a soft hand nudged, then leaned heavily on my shoulder.

"What the—?"

A jean-clad butt pressed against me and sat on the same log. A blonde head took the place of the hand on my shoulder, and dark, arched eyebrows over silver blue eyes looked up at me.

"Hey, stranger."

Patricia.

With a full glass of beer in one hand, she began singing loudly and enthusiastically, even though neither Barry nor I was playing.

She didn't care. She was having fun just creating her own melody and words.

I had fun too. Even though I knew she was drunk, I loved the warmth of her body next to mine.

Then, across the fire, I spotted Alf.

This was not good. Totally inconvenient.

Ignore him. Distract yourself, I told myself.

I pounded out an annoying waltz beat on my guitar to match her improvised song, belting out my harmony and lyrics.

Eventually, the song ended. Laughter and cheers echoed through the woods and across the water. Now would be a good time to leave.

Before I could stand, however, Patricia laid her head on my shoulder and patted my cheek.

Oh, Lord! Alf, you can't see this. Don't see this. I panicked as my head swiveled, hunting for Patricia's boyfriend.

There he was, still across the fire with a mug of beer in his big hands, one foot perched on an empty log. I didn't remember him being so big.

I tried to move, but Patricia leaned harder against me.

Alarmed and dumbfounded, I attempted to wriggle away. A small, soft hand grabbed my shirt and pulled me back. Her nose close to mine, Patricia slurred, "Michael, do you like me?"

Words wouldn't form on my lips or on my tongue or in my throat.

Of course, I *liked* her. I'd always *liked* her. This was my chance to tell her I LOVED her. But right then was not the time.

There was Alf across the fire, watching us, waiting for my answer more than Patricia was. I had to leave. Fast!

That's ridiculous, I rationalized. *He couldn't have heard us.*

But I knew he had.

What could I say?

I looked down first at her wet, shiny blue eyes. Had she been crying? Why was she crying?

I glanced down at her hand and her glass of beer. I cleared my throat and squeaked, "Do I like you? Yeah. Usually."

She leaned back curiously. "Usually? How about now?"

Alf stepped steadily toward us.

I shook my head.

"No?" Patricia winced. "Why not?"

I pursed my lips.

She grimaced. "Is it because I'm drunk?"

Alf stood over us, as confused as his girlfriend was.

Patricia's face darkened. "It's my boyfriend, isn't it?"

I shook my head and exhaled. "It's because you're pouring beer inside my guitar."

Alf roared with laughter and knelt next to Patricia, wrapping an arm around her. "Good answer," he said, offering me his beer. "Here. Have a drink."

All the times we had talked at the coffeehouse, I had always sought his approval to get closer to Patricia. However, whether or not I took a beer had nothing to do with her.

It just wasn't right.

You can do this. Just say no. *Just say* no.

I shook my head.

"No, really. Here. Try it," he said, shoving his glass in my face.

His unrelenting smirk reminded me of the father I had never known—what he had done to my mother, my grandfather.

I didn't want his beer. I just wanted to go home.

"Come on. Drink it." Alf's harsh, unflinching voice silenced the crowd.

Under his arm, Patricia squirmed. She eyes pleaded with me, "Take the glass."

In that moment I had two overwhelming truths I had to face: First, I didn't want his beer. Second, even though I wanted his girlfriend, I couldn't do this.

"I...uh... I don't—I don't drink," I stammered.

Astounded, both Alf and Patricia turned on my roommate Barry.

"Really?" Alf asked.

Barry nodded and began packing his guitar. "He never has."

The couple turned their stare on me. I flailed my arms helplessly, looking for words, but again, I was speechless. I could not hide the conflict in my eyes.

Patricia's face softened. She understood.

She laid her hand on Alf's arm, smiled at me, and said, "He doesn't need to. He's goofy enough without it. Let's go."

The crowd around us relaxed as the two stood, an arm around each other's waist, and walked away. I sat with my hands lying limply on my lap while Patricia and Alf disappeared into the brush.

"You okay?" Barry asked me as he snapped his guitar case shut.

I thought for a second. *Have a beer or lose any chance with Patricia. I had a choice and I had been strong enough to say no.*

I looked off into the woods, then and up the cliff where the party had disappeared. "I'm fine," I said as I packed my guitar.

"One good thing," Barry said as the two of us kicked sand into the fire.

"What's that?"

"The next time somebody asks why you don't drink, you've got the perfect line."

"What's that?"

"You're goofy enough without it."

I laughed and picked up my guitar. Goofy integrity was better than breaking a vow.

"Shut up. Let's go home."

Chopping Down Cherry Trees

"WE LEARNED ABOUT HONESTY and integrity - that the truth matters... that you don't take shortcuts or play by your own set of rules... and success doesn't count unless you earn it fair and square."

Michelle Obama

One of our first lessons in honesty and integrity—the one that states "Truth matters"—comes in elementary school when we are taught one of the most ironic stories in American history, George Washington and the cherry tree.

For those of you who have forgotten, the story goes that as a boy George was out playing with a hatchet he had received as a gift.

As boys do.

In an enthusiastic test of the implement's sharpness plus his own strength and chopping ability, George whacked down his father's cherry tree. When confronted by his father, he supposedly stood up straight and bravely confessed, "I cannot tell a lie. I cut down that cherry tree."

The lesson we were to take home was that "honesty is the best policy," that yes, telling the truth has consequences, but not as dire as sacrificing one's integrity.

Later, we discovered that in all likelihood there was no hatchet, no chopping, and not even a cherry tree, that this story meant to teach the value of truth was in fact false. In the long run, we learned that despite the good aims, integrity is more the result of a single life-altering experience than a hundred well-intentioned fables. In addition, success doesn't come from how many legends you encounter or slogans you can repeat. It comes from good character earned fairly and squarely by assimilating the principles of honesty and fairness. Success outside the rules of the game is not winning; it's just getting what you want.

Most often, getting what you want hurts more than losing.

One of the dangers of becoming a high school English teacher—or any teacher for that matter—is the inclination to view yourself as all-seeing, all-knowing, to claim wisdom far above not only your adolescent students, but their parents, their employers, and even their pet salamander Spot. Match that egotism against a hormonal imbalance that tells a fifteen-year-old, pimply-faced, squeaky-voiced farm boy he really doesn't need to read that Shakespeare guy to grow potatoes —Well, there are going to be problems.

Especially when you're so angry you forget all the statistics, details, and suggestions you learned in human development class, the instruction that warned you to face conflict with virtue and decency immediately, up front, calmly, not allowing passions to grow. The advice that promised by doing so, the dispute would be shorter with milder consequences. The lessons that advocated abandoning your pride, discarding the revenge of making the student suffer, and avoiding the surrender of your authority to somebody else—like the principal. The guidance that told you in cases of conflict to trust what you know is right to manage the situation by yourself.

Early in my career, my classroom authority was pretty much all show. I learned all the right words, but I had not experienced the actions I should implement. I'd like to say I was young and inexperienced—I was—but the truth is I was a blustering pinhead.

I should have seen the moment coming. All the signs were there, but my arrogance blinded me. This scruffily dressed, lanky ninth grader—Richard "Woody" Woodward —came in the first day and began tearing apart the curriculum before I got through the first bullet point of the syllabus. By the second week, this nitwit chewed up and spit aside the contention that knowledge of your native language and familiarity with its literature is anything more than a grand plot to squelch freedom and inner harmony.

Woody never used those words. He wouldn't have known what they meant. Besides, he didn't need "no fancy words." At 14-years-old, he was a "man of action," intent on asserting his dominance over authority. Especially mine.

The first few weeks were just training for him, minor sparring, with Woody jabbing and weaving in preparation for the battle royal to come. He simple bided his time until I broke.

It didn't take long.

When the day finally came, he was on a mission to crush me. From the moment the bell rang and I had taken attendance, no matter what I tried to say, skepticism became sneers. Sarcasm became scorn. Irritating pencil drumming became books dropped on the floor.

And then the little turd blossom smiled at me—SMILED —daring me to do something.

My insides exploded.

Everything I had ever learned in textbooks and lectures —the counsel, the warnings, the techniques—vanished. The veins in my neck stiffened. Blood rushed to my cheeks. I ranted. I raved. I flailed.

And Woody? He leaned back in his chair, spread his legs into the aisle, and SMILED AGAIN, thoroughly enjoying himself. He had me and he knew it.

I knew it too, but I couldn't show it. Instead, I stomped

to the door, swung it open, and blabbered something incomprehensible even to me.

"What?" he said, snickering.

He and the whole class eagerly awaited my answer.

I flexed my fists, shook my head, and wiped the spit from my mouth with my forearm. "Get out!" I screeched.

The class laughed. The boy smirked.

I cleared my throat and repeated in a growl, "Get out."

"Where do you want me to go?" he said.

"I—I—I don't care. Just get out."

He shrugged, stood, walked past me, and clenched both hands victoriously over his head to the class as he left the room.

The defiance shocked even his classmates. The entire class gawked at me, waiting for my reaction, but I didn't have any. What was I supposed to do? Still they waited. "Do something," their silent, gaping mouths commanded.

They were right. I was in charge, so I slammed the door and tromped after him, leaving behind a classroom of bewildered and exasperated teenagers. (Yes, that was stupid. I know that NOW!)

I found him slumped in the waiting room chair in the principal's office, as I should have. He was obviously familiar with office protocol—*Kicked out of class? Go to the office and wait.* Before I could restart the confrontation, the secretary opened the principal's door and announced, "He's waiting for you."

I swerved around Woody's long legs stretched out to block me, barged into the office, and explained the situation to the principal. The ex-Marine leapt from his desk, marched to the door, and shouted at the culprit, "RICHARD! Get in here."

Woody rose awkwardly, furtively looking for an escape route. There was none. Feigning nonchalance, he shuffled into the office, but he knew he was in trouble.

Lots of trouble.

Within seconds of interrogation and berating, the

principal reduced him to a blubbering puddle of snot and tears before flinging him back to the waiting room and slamming the door.

The room was silent. No sound outside the door, nothing inside.

The principal smiled and said softly, "Is that what you wanted?"

I grinned and nodded, victoriously.

He shook his head, walked across the room and sat on his desk before me. "No, it isn't," he said. "Sit down."

Taking the chair Woody had just left, I wilted under the principal's gaze. He was a short man, but still menacing. He stood before me, his head bent, his arms crossing his chest, his eyes glowering. "You screwed up, Michael," he stated unemotionally.

Stunned, I grasped at the thousands of words swirling around my brain. Only one emerged from my mouth. "How?"

"You sent him here. I have nothing to do with this situation. It's all between you and him.

"And you know what else? It isn't over. By sending him to me, you just postponed the inevitable. The two of you are going to have to work this out between you. And you need to do it soon. You know that. Right?"

Of course, he was right. I squirmed under his glare, then admitted, "I don't know what to do."

"Yes, you do. You're not a dummy."

I felt like one.

"Think."

So I thought. And thought. The answers were clear. I nodded.

"Tell me. What are you going to do?"

"Talk to him. Apologize."

"For what?"

"For overreacting. For not listening to him. For sending him here."

The principal laughed. "You can forget that last part.

He's been here a lot. He's used to me. He'll be here again. What about the class?"

"I should apologize to them as well?"

He shook his head. "They don't need to hear you say you're sorry. They need you to say you were wrong."

"Was I wrong?"

He nodded vigorously.

Of course, I was, but I needed to ask. "Why tell them?"

"Because you were. And you'll be wrong again. They already know that, but they need to hear you say it. They need to know you're human, that you make mistakes, and that you value their opinion of you. They don't need you to scare them; they need you to like them. Then move on."

I had actually written those words in my notes for teaching methods class. I had forgotten the most fundamental rule of the course: Life's real lessons aren't words on a page. Until you live them, they are just legends and myths like George Washington chopping down the cherry tree. Only when they are put into practice are they worth anything.

What are the lessons I just learned, the lessons I need to live by? I wondered. The answers didn't take long to arrive.

Do what needs to be done. Be honest. Tell the truth. Love those students. Be a teacher.

I stood and shook the principal's hand. "Thanks, " I said. "I will."

Earning respect is hard. It's a lifelong struggle for integrity— for PHIL— and there is no easy way. Pawning off responsibilities on somebody else is not an option. No, you make your mistakes, you admit them, and you fix them. It's the only way of becoming what you want to be.

Years later, I heard Michelle Obama describe her own growth experience this way: "We learned about honesty and integrity—that the truth matters...that you don't take shortcuts or play by your own set of rules...and success doesn't count unless you earn it fair and square."

As she suggested—and what life teaches—success is

more multidimensional than simply getting what you desire. It means that all the stumbles and restarts, conviction and repentance, and even outright failures have finally created a more complete you, an authentic you. Not just who you wanted to be, but who you were always meant to be.

More than Success

"IF I WERE ASKED to say the most important things that lead to a successful life, I should say that, first of all, was integrity - unimpeachable integrity."
Charles M. Schwab

Few would dispute that Charles Schwab led a successful life or that his reputation, at least by biographers' standards, is a stellar example of integrity. Still the definition of the terms *successful life* and *unimpeachable integrity* can be debated.

One definition of *success* is "the attainment of wealth, position, honors or the like." Unfortunately, for many, that definition is as far as they think the term goes. To them, success is always measured in money, title, medals, and so on. In other words, stuff. However, Schwab's addition of *unimpeachable integrity* adds the spiritual components of right, truth, and commitment to a higher goal, which sometimes results in saying no to something you really want. Sometimes it means admitting you're wrong. Sometimes it means LOSING and gaining something far better than gold or a job.

By adding integrity to the definition, success can actually be accomplishing an objective through sheer will, effort, and sincerity that neither you or anybody else thought you could.

Like Nanako did.

Nanako was a Japanese foreign exchange student raised

in an intense urban environment who had been thrust into a Scandinavian, rural Minnesota town. Like her foreign exchange predecessors, she was anxious to learn about America, but she was also eager to share about her home country.

While intelligent and well read, Nanako was also very shy, an insecurity brought on by her limited English skills. However, while her black-haired Asian features stuck out in a sea of blonde Norskes, she was determined to blend in with the student body and to make the most of her experience, not just in the classroom but in extra-curricular activities. Unfortunately, in our small school, her choices were limited since she had few athletic skills.

Which led her to the speech team.

A team member had told her about the category of informative speaking where she could utilize not only her speaking skills, but also her artistic abilities to develop visual aids. Plus, she could teach her audiences about Japan, comparing the education system there to what she was experiencing in America.

Which led her to the coach. Me.

Our first session revealed a strength of character I had seldom seen in new competitors. While her verbal English skills were problematic for such a language-intensive activity, she wrote well and challenged herself to overcome her obstacles. She bravely accepted her limitations and realistically decided winning was not her goal. That would be frustrating. Instead, no matter what problems she encountered, she would do whatever she could to become a better English speaker.

Her problems began on Day One of practice when she brought in her rough draft. Instructed to find a good teaser to catch her audience's attention, she had combed through source after source to find a catchy phrase or story with the right amount of humor and context to captivate her listeners.

As luck would have it, she happened upon one of best quotations to describe the bustling life in both America and

Japan: "The trouble with the rat race is that even if you win you're still a rat." When she described what she had to do for her Japanese education—the daily train rides, the after-school classes, the testing—those words were the perfect lead-in for her subject.

They were not perfect for her tongue.

You know the stereotype about Japanese people mixing up their Ls and Rs when they try to learn English? Often it's true. That's why it's a stereotype. It was especially true for Nanako.

Her great capture statement went from "The trouble with the rat race is that even if you win you're still a rat" into "The trouber with the lat lace is that even if you win you'll stir a lat."

"That's not going to work," I told her, but she was unshakeable that she could learn the pronunciation.

So she tried. And tried. And tried.

Day after day. Week after week. Until the first invitational contest where not one judge commented on her accent. At least in the intro. That was a relief.

"However," one judge wrote, "you failed to cite the source of your quote."

Now she was in real trouble. The person who originally said those words?

Lily Tomlin.

Yes.

Or as Nanako said, "Riry Tomrin."

Still, she claimed as all her coaches had told her, it was a long season. She would learn.

And she did.

However, her tongue didn't always remember from one round to the next.

She remained undaunted and became moderately successful over all the tournaments. *Success* meaning she didn't always come in last.

Was she disappointed? Yes, but her "unimpeachable integrity" kept her at work all season long until the elimination season, which began with the district competition.

On the bus ride to the contest, we coaches explained to her that only four people in each category would advance to the next level, so her chances were not real good. She already knew that, but felt she had already succeeded. She was better than when the season began. She was happy. When the bus pulled up at the contest site, she thanked us, gathered her materials, climbed down the steps, squeezed though the narrow doors, and hustled across the icy path to speak.

That was the last her teammates or coaches saw of her until the awards ceremony. The outcome was certain in our eyes. Nobody expected her to advance. Not even Nanako herself. Still, we were proud of her. She had accomplished far more than anybody had expected.

And then...

After all the speakers had finished competing, six finalists in each category stood in the center of the gym floor to receive their placings. Four would advance to regions the next week.

"To keep the ceremony moving smoothly, please withhold any clapping until the awards in each category are finished," the announcer requested. For the first five categories, the audience complied with her instructions.

Then came informative speaking. The finalists moved forward. Including Nanako. The whole gym gasped.

Our team squirmed excitedly, covering their mouths with one hand and sitting on the other to prevent any inadvertent applause. Even though the category was small, NANAKO WAS A FINALIST. That was more than anybody in the whole district had anticipated.

At the center court circle, the six speakers lined up, adjusted their posture, and looked to the announcer to begin. The announcer hesitated, glanced at me, and smiled.

"What's that all about?" the student next to me asked.

"I have no idea."

Slowly, to build the suspense, the announcer began:

"Sixth place, the second alternate to regions…"

Hearts jumped and voices squeaked. The team never heard the name. They just knew it was not Nanako. They grabbed hands and leaned toward the floor.

"Well, that's cool," we coaches whispered to each other. "Not last in finals. Good."

"Fifth place, first alternate to regions…"

The announcer's pause was too long.

She spoke, but again, nobody heard the name. We just knew once again it was not Nanako.

The team gasped. "That means…"

At center court, Nanako covered her mouth with her hands. Her knees quivered.

"In fourth place, advancing to the regional tournament…"

Nanako's shoulders shook. Her face twisted and tightened.

She knew.

She was advancing.

She sank to her knees, tears of joy streaming down her face. Laughing and cheering, her competitors encircled her, hugged her, and lifted her so she could receive her award.

She raised her head, light sparkling off the tears on her face, her mouth gasping for breath.

Fourth place was more than "success" for her, more than stuff. It was pure elation. Through months of practice, defeat, and frustration, she had stayed true to the purpose of the activity, to her goal, to herself.

Today, that ribbon is probably lost and ignored at the bottom of a drawer somewhere in Japan, but that doesn't matter. That night, as Nanako entered the bus to her teammates' cheers, her life was successful. More than any gold medal or trophy, she had won what she could never lose. Unimpeachable integrity.

There Is a Point

"INTEGRITY HAS NO NEED of rules."
Albert Camus

Two of the most irritating phrases teachers and parents hear when teaching their kids about self-discipline is "What for? What's in it for me?" Somewhere the idea of behavior being dependent on reward and/or punishment has become engrained in our collective psyche.

Call it the Santa Claus Effect.

Be good; get a present...or eighty. Be bad; get a lump of coal stuffed into a musty old sock...or lutefisk for Christmas dinner. As long as there's an elf on the shelf spying on them, children are model offspring, picking up the dishes and their toys, always saying thank you, and feeding the cat—even if you don't have a cat. However, when they don't think anybody's paying attention, they pinch and fart and slobber while making their worst googly eyes about Grandma's whiskers.

As they get older, when the material connection to behavior becomes more tenuous, the innocent question *What for?* turns to the ominous *What's the point?*

Something was wrong.
It was 6:30 in the morning. The hall outside my

classroom should have been empty. That's why I came to work so early. Not to show off my dedication, but to ease into the day, a day beginning with peace and quiet, slowly morphing into busy-ness.

But this day in the still-nighttime lighting, Silas, a quiet senior, had already invaded my space, sitting cross-legged and leaning against my door, appearing small, almost shrunken.

"Strange place for a nap," I joked.

"Couldn't sleep at home," he muttered.

"So you came to school? I'm not sure what that says about the job we're doing."

He uncurled, stood, then moved aside to let me unlock my room. Gazing at the floor, he pulled on the back of his neck. Neither of us said a word as I turned on the light and entered. *I'm losing my touch*, I thought.

As I hung up my jacket, Silas wandered aimlessly through the rows of desks, his eyes unfocused, his fingers trailing over the desktops. "You okay?" I asked.

He hesitated, wary and almost disappointed. "You didn't hear," he mumbled as he sat at a desk.

"Hear what?"

He twisted his shoulders, struggling to release the words that dribbled out between stifled sobs.

"Tom…suicide…hanging…"

I pushed back my chair. My mouth hung open. *No, that can't be*, I thought. *Tom? No. My Tom? Tom from the speech team? No way. He graduated. He's happy. This can't be true.*

One glance at Silas hunched forward, hugging the desktop, confirmed it was.

Of course. They were best friends.

Defying the rising sun outside, darkness engulfed the room. I leaned back in my chair and struggled for breath, still denying reality.

Across the aisle, I saw Silas's swollen eyes gazing at me, waiting, pleading, for what I did not know. His quivering cheeks revealed the reason. He ached for comfort, for words of wisdom and solace, anything to to help him deal with this crushing reality. He wasn't there just to tell me; he needed me. He needed his teacher.

But at that moment, I could not be a teacher. I had no wisdom. I had no words.

None.

Tom was more than a student. He was one of my kids.

I wanted to run. I wanted to scream.

The door opened. Judy, a classmate and friend, wandered in shakily and sat next to Silas to share the space. Neither spoke.

Slowly, one by one, the room filled with distraught students—classmates, underclassmen, boys and girls alike. Curious staff—teachers, custodians, aides—peeked in to check out the gathering throng. Whispered questions filled the room.

"What happened?"

"Who?"

"No! Why?"

Girls cried. Boys hugged.

Nobody had answers, least of all me.

I sat quietly behind my desk, my lips pressed tightly together. College had not taught us how to deal with this, how to endure, what to say, how to do our jobs and still be human.

Somewhere, the time flew and the room became a blur.

The warning bell rattled the walls and windows.

Five minutes until class.

Class.

How was that going to work? Who wanted to learn about independent clauses or comma splices or *Of Mice and Men* today?

Who was going to teach them?

Logic suggested that lessons might distract us all from our grief, but as true as that might be…

Some students left. Those in my first period took out their materials and prepared for class. Stragglers in the hall shuffled in and took their seats.

The bell rang.

I sighed and took attendance. Nobody spoke.

A voice on the intercom broke the silence. The principal.

Rather than glossing over or obscuring the news, he confronted the truth, explaining what was certain so far. He also acknowledged the emotions students may be experiencing and announced that if they needed grief counseling, town clergy and school psychologists would be available in the cafeteria. He urged friends of the victim to take advantage of the opportunity, but encouraged all others to continue with their studies as usual.

Which meant teachers were to continue as usual.

As usual.

There was nothing usual about this morning. We were as lost as the kids.

Some students exited and others remained as they had been instructed. Somehow those of us left muddled through, and first period ended. That class exited while the reduced ranks of period two filed in silently. Dutiful and obedient, they slid into their desks, although it was obvious nobody wanted to be there. Some were weary of telling the story, while others were tired of hearing it.

Personally, I was tired of everything and everybody. I wanted to go home, wrap myself up in a blanket and crank Beatles songs for hours.

Or days.

I wasn't sure if being alone was a good idea, either. I had failed Tom. I had failed Silas and all his friends. I had failed as a teacher. What was the point of being in school?

A knock on the classroom door jarred my thoughts.

Through the window, I saw David Livingston, my pastor, standing next to Ellen, an off-duty science teacher. I opened the door and peeked out my head. "What's going on?" I asked in hushed tones.

Ellen answered, "Talk to Pastor Dave. I'll watch your class." She walked past me and closed the door behind her.

I was lost in an empty hallway.

Dave looked at me and held my arm. "How are you doing?"

I shrugged away the pain in my belly. "I'm okay, I guess. I thought you were talking to the kids."

He nodded. "I was. Just finished. That's why I'm here."

"What do you mean?"

"As we finished, I asked them if they were all right or if there was anybody else who should have been at the meeting. They all looked at each other and said they would be fine, but Mr. Frickstad could use some help."

He wrapped me in his arms and whispered, "They want to make sure you're all right. You're special to them."

Those words and Dave's embrace got me through the day, but the rest of the week was a blur. I know I prayed a lot. Prayed that I could help the kids, help the boy's family. Prayed that I could find answers.

I waited and found none. Even throughout the funeral, I listened for truth, for solace, for direction, for words to relay to Tom's family and friends.

"Please, tell me something," I begged inside. "Something that just... Just tell me why I'm here. What am I supposed to be doing?"

I was so busy talking, I forgot to listen.

After the last hymn was sung, the last blessing pronounced over the congregation, and the casket rolled out of the sanctuary, the answer still eluded me.

Frustrated, I rose and shuffled to the side door to avoid people. Across the street, members of the speech team clumped together, the same people with whom Tom once joked and debated.

I should join them, I thought, but I wasn't up for reminiscing. I needed to be alone. I ignored them.

I ducked my head, slipped out the door, turned sharply at the sidewalk, and strode toward the school, my shoes clacking on the broken concrete.

Something didn't feel right.

I slowed, then looked up at the strangely clear sky. The blankness frustrated me. There was nothing to stop the transmission of God's answer, so why couldn't I hear Him?

No, I was beyond frustrated. I was angry.

My brain shouted to the blue, *Okay, God, it's just you and me. Why am I here? What's the point? Tell me! Not later. Now!*

From the other side of the street, a voice called, "We love you, Mr. F."

I glanced up and saw the students huddled together, watching me.

Tears welled in my eyes as I lowered them to my feet to avoid the cracks in the sidewalk. I couldn't look up.

Okay. I get it.

I raised an arm and called back, "I love you, too."

It had been a dark, horrible week. The future looked far brighter.

I wish I could say things got better, that we—teachers, students, town—lived happily ever after, but we didn't. After that horrible incident, sociologists warned us there could be an epidemic. Be prepared.

They were right.

But nobody could tell us how to stop it. All the professionals had theories—medical, emotional, religious, philosophical—none of which eased the torment. Too many opinions, too few solutions.

And still students came to us adults for answers that none of us had. They were like three-year-olds pleading the same naggingly incessant question.

The same one we asked ourselves.

Why?

We tried our best to answer.

To no avail.

After the third funeral, students mobbed my classroom.

"Mr. F! That Dork Head said Lonnie is in hell! Is he in hell?"

The words stunned me. I could not force myself to go to the funeral so I hadn't heard them. I sat back in my chair, my mouth gaping.

If what the students said was true, Lonnie's minister was a real dork head...although I had cruder names to call him. How could anybody say that to a fragile congregation of family and adolescents? How could anybody be so cold, so calloused? No matter how true he thought his words were, those kids needed comfort, not condemnation. They needed living words.

Red, contorted faces raged around me. "What do you think, Mr. F? Is Lonnie in hell?"

I sighed.

Back in college, I had heard those same sentiments expressed in late-night dorm discussions, listened to the theological rationale, even nodded at the fear-based tactic of "scaring the hell" out of suicide survivors.

However, now, in my classroom, the concept was not a vague hypothetical, but instead a cold reality. That afternoon, the words had not been spoken by a group of college thinkers contemplating reality, but by an authoritarian spouting out a practiced twisting of scripture that ignored the love of Christ. These students—unwitting casualties of Dork Head's heartless reasoning—rejected the rash human damnation of their friend. They resented any adult who could hold that opinion. They came to me, some for confirmation of their feelings, some to challenge my faith, some just because they were so conflicted they needed to hear somebody else's truth.

The words were out of my mouth before I even thought them.

"I don't think so. No."

Given my opinions of long ago, the words surprised me, but they were honest.

"Why not?"

I felt stuck.

Were those the right words?

My answer was purely speculative. I had no scriptural

evidence, no logical analysis, no witty proverb. There was only one correct answer to their *why not.*

"I don't know. It's what I believe."

The group thought quietly.

Finally, Hope, a short-haired brunette who had barely spoken all year, murmured, "Me too."

Slowly, all the others nodded. They didn't need to agree with the minister. They didn't have to agree with me. They just needed to believe what they believed. That was enough.

"Thanks, Mr. F," they said as they left the room.

Knowing what you believe is the most important step to integrity, but living what you believe is the hardest. It's easier when you know why. Life *is* worth living, but not for money or sex or food or power or fame or praise. In fact, by eliminating integrity, the Santa Claus Effect is more apt to destroy life than develop it.

As I write this, there are 7.7 billion different people on this planet, each with our own body, our own abilities, our own perspective, our own voice. We each live, learn, share, and most importantly, love one another, spreading that love to whom we can, whenever and wherever we can—the way only each one of us can.

During those gut-wrenching weeks, I learned that truth from my students, their actions, their concerns, and their words. Their integrity.

Their PHIL to my flop.

Absurdists like Camus may think integrity has no need of rules, but unlike their philosophy, it does have to have a point—far more than the threat of any punishment or the promise of any reward. By providing a foundation for peace, hope and love, integrity makes life worth living.

<u>Love</u>

Gaylord's Wish

"LOVE IS FRIENDSHIP THAT has caught fire. It is quiet understanding, mutual confidence, sharing and forgiving. It is loyalty through good and bad times. It settles for less than perfection and makes allowances for human weaknesses."

Ann Landers

At one time in my life—maybe in everybody's life—it was really easy to separate the emotions of liking and loving. You liked your friends; you loved your mother.

Or your significant other.

Or whoever you wanted to be your significant other.

Or your mother.

Other than that, in conversation, you saved the word *love* for the "forever" ones in your life.

I waited until I was 24.

Until that time I had had one steady girlfriend, which made claiming to be an expert on relationships wrong on so many levels. But that didn't stop me from expressing my ignorance.

I remember when I first heard Lobo's song "Don't Expect Me to Be Your Friend," especially the chorus's last two lines: "I love you too much to ever start liking you, so don't expect me to be your friend."

I thought, *The man is a genius. I have to tell everybody I know.*

I mean that's what life is all about. Right? Especially romance? Love or nothing. Who doesn't agree with that?

I quickly found out quite a few people.

Once again, a late-night dorm discussion resulted, quickly turning into a heated commentary on the accuracy of that assertion.

In the midst of the evening bedlam, one of my supporters shouted, "Lobo's right. Liking is less than loving!"

"No, he's not. You think you can really love somebody without liking them?" others countered. "Think about what the guy's singing: 'Friendship is weaker than love.' Do you really believe that?"

"He doesn't say that. He says—"

"Yes, he does. 'Don't expect me to be your friend. I want to be your lover.'"

At which point, a calmer voice—mine—broke in, slowly stretching out the obvious truth: "Because...friendship— especially between the sexes—is...BORING!".

Long-frustrated by romantic intentions, I still held to the belief that amorous love was, without a doubt, the epitome of human emotions. Nobody was going to change my mind.

Until the dorm floor's sole music major interrupted the conversation. "No, no, no. Come on. You guys are missing the most important question. It has nothing to do with liking and loving."

"So what's the most important question then?"

"Why would a guy change his name to the Spanish word for *wolf*, then write such a hokey song?"

In retrospect, I was really stupid. Still enslaved by the ravages of late-onset puberty, I didn't know a thing about life, love, or anything else for that matter. My pathetic romantic relationships had been ones of ignorance and frustration with only occasional sparks of elation and acceptance.

Why? Because I had failed to recognize a fundamental

truth of affection: Love is love.

That's it.

Love is love.

Basic and simple.

No degrees. No shades.

When Lobo divided friends and lovers implying that only lovers love, that at best, friends only like, he was not a genius; he was ridiculous. The need for friendship and love is instinctive, and he should have known that. Even a guy raised in the north woods had already learned that years before in elementary school.

I forgot.

In second grade, my favorite part of the school day was not art or phys ed or morning milk. It was Show and Tell, that introduction to public speaking where students stood before the class and shared their favorite toy, memory, or talent. Everybody's interests and stuff were so unique, I could hardly wait to hear what made each person tick.

Some girls brought dolls and drawings, while some boys brought baseball bats and toy soldiers. Some people obviously practiced and almost jumped out of their desks raising their hands to go first, while others—those great at improvisation—waited for the three-second lag after the teacher's call "Next."

Some demonstrations were serious, some were funny, and some—particularly those who waited beyond the first two groups—were mistakes.

I felt sorry for them.

Every day, there were those who sat on their hands until nobody was left. They weren't rebellious. They usually said they forgot or claimed they had nothing to share. The rest of us knew they were scared and would probably pee their pants if they got up in front of everybody.

We almost wished they would. At least that would be funny.

One particular morning, Mrs. Lindval, a scrawny, short-

haired woman with owl-head glasses and a constant scowl—
a woman we called Mrs. Grumpy Puss—stood and barked
the dreaded words, "Who hasn't presented yet?"

We early speakers sat smugly and proudly, our backs a
little straighter and our smirks a little wider. Our heads
swiveled as our eyes searched the room for delinquents we
could belittle—the shy, the lazy, the punks, the ones who
usually ducked their heads under folded arms on their desks.

But today had been a busy day. As I searched the room, I
couldn't remember any obvious slackers. Not even—

Oh, wait.

Gaylord.

The puny, bashful boy with a head full of cowlicks and
the voice of a chipmunk who sat in the last seat in the row
closest to the window. Nobody ever paid attention to him
there. It was a perfect place to daydream and hide.

Except that morning. We all knew who the only person
left was. He couldn't hide from all of us. As I turned to point
him out to Mrs. Grumpy Puss, I realized I had never seen him
do Show and Tell before. Certainly not this year, but not even
in first grade. What could be better than watching him do a
real Show and Tell? Watching how he would get out of it this
time.

The air vibrated as the collective attention of the class
focused on Gaylord, the faded plaid shirt and scuffed jeans
he wore every day, and his trembling chin. Under the
excruciating scrutiny, he brushed his long greasy hair from
his eyes and glanced nervously at the cute girls, the bully
boys, and grim-faced teacher. He sighed deeply, planted his
chin on his chest and slowly raised his hand.

"Gaylord. Good," Mrs. Lindval said. "What did you
bring to share?"

Yeah, I thought. *What? You never have anything?*

He mumbled incomprehensibly.

"What was that?" Mrs. Lindval demanded.

In a tiny little voice, he said, "A wish."

We kids all looked at each other, then quickly at the

teacher. Could he do that?

She adjusted the glasses on her nose and examined him. Her voice softened. "Oh. All right. Go ahead," she replied, lowering herself into the chair behind her desk.

Gaylord hid his eyes and slunk to the front of the room. He took a look at the taped presenter's circle on the floor, bit his lip, and stepped into it, his narrow fingers silently drumming the table next to him.

"Be nice and loud," Mrs. Lindval encouraged.

"I wish…" he whispered.

"Louder!" Bruce the Bully barked.

The class roared.

"Bruce!" Mrs. Lindval snapped, pulling off her glasses, her electric eyes crackling. "You know better. And so do the rest of you."

The room was silent.

The little boy in the circle licked his lips, clasped his hands behind him, and swung his hips from side to side.

"Go ahead, Gaylord," Mrs. Lindval said softly. She almost smiled, confusing the class. We had never seen a pleasant expression on her face.

Gaylord took a deep breath, gulped, and stammered, "I w-w-wish…"

He took another deep breath and forced himself to finish. "I wish I had friends."

Hesitating a moment to glance at Mrs. Lindval, he lowered his head and scurried back to his desk. He laid his head in his arms facing the window.

His words shook the classroom. Nobody could speak, not even Mrs. Lindval.

She just stared at Gaylord, the hushed class, and the books on her desk. Slowly, she stood reaching for her arithmetic book and a pile of papers.

"Um… Okay. That was the last one. Thank you all for sharing. Everybody take out your math…er…arithmetic book…turn to page 37, then do these subtraction worksheets. When you're finished, raise your hands and I'll pick them up."

The girl in front of me held the worksheets over her shoulder for me to take and pass back. I did so, then turned to the sheet on my desk, wondering how many and what kind of problems we had today.

Fifteen problems. Subtraction.

Oh, yeah. She said that.

All three-digit numbers.

I immediately forgot Show and Tell. We had never even added three-digits before. Subtraction was harder.

From the corner of my eye, I watched Gaylord's unmoving head. He wiped his mouth with his shirt. He always hated arithmetic.

Slowly, I raised my hand. "Mrs. Lindval?"

"Yes?"

"Isn't that a lot of problems? We've never…"

"Yeah," Bruce chimed in. "Fricky's right. We ain't never done this kinda—

The teacher threw up her hands and slammed them on her desk. "JUST—"

Student desks rattled as the class jumped. A girl screeched. Books tumbled to the floor. Startled, trembling boys pushed back from their desks.

Mrs Lindval raised her hands and caught her breath.

"Just… Just do the best you can."

Heads lowered en masse. In the quiet, papers shuffled, pencils scratched.

Mrs. Lindval rose from her desk, her commanding lips pulled tight against her teeth as she moved through the rows watching us work. As she brushed by me, her fingers stretched and relaxed, stretched and relaxed, almost guiltily.

In the back corner by the window, she stopped next to Gaylord, who had not moved. She rubbed his back as she picked up his pencil. She wrapped his fingers around it, then whispered in his ear. He looked up at her. She nodded, handed him a tissue, then tapped the worksheet.

He wiped his eyes, blew his nose, then began to attack

the mystery of subtracting numbers he could never count to.

What happened next?
I don't know.
Something.
I do know that as the year went on, students sat with Gaylord at assemblies, helped him with his arithmetic and art, and made sure he had a seat at lunch.

I know Bruce the Bully left him alone.

And Mrs. Lindval smiled at him.

And us.

We never called her Mrs. Grumpy Puss again.

Whatever she told Gaylord that day, his school life changed. He had friends. Not many, but enough to make him happy. Loyal, supportive friends who accepted him, talked to him, laughed with him, cared for him. Friends who liked him.

Friends who loved him.

When I heard Lobo's song years later, I should have remembered Gaylord. His seven-year-old brain didn't concern itself with definitions or any artificial concepts of *like* and *love*. When he wished for a friend, he didn't need a wolf-man (Lobo) to confuse him. What he wanted, what he needed, was simply love. Because love is all.

PHIL reminds us that love created the universe and all of humanity. Love sustains us. It is the greatest gift from God.

Ever.

Part of the Deal

"BEING DEEPLY LOVED BY someone gives you strength, while loving someone deeply gives you courage."
Lao Tzu

"So what do I call him?"

"Who?"

"Ernie."

"What do you mean?"

"Well, he still won't be my father, will he? Not really."

My mom sat down in front of me. "Let me explain something. When Ernie asked me to marry him, I told him he'd be marrying you, too."

"What did he say?"

"He said he always knew you'd be part of the deal. He loves me. He loves you. 'Real father,' or not."

My short, skinny body fidgeted.

Adjusting to the idea of life with a step-father is difficult for an eight-year-old. You want your mother to be happy, but you also want her for yourself. Yes, the idea of a father is great, but then all of a sudden, reality hits. She's marrying this guy....

"Can I just still call him Ernie?"

"You don't want to call him Dad?"

"Yeah, I do, but...I don't know."

She stroked my head and smiled. "Okay. When you get to know him better. When it's right. I'll explain it to him. He'll understand."

When we all moved in together, things were so different, I knew saying *Dad* was going to take awhile.

When Mom and I lived with Grandma and Grandpa, it was in the largest house in town. (It wasn't really. I was just so puny, it seemed that way.) With Ernie, we lived in a small cabin in the middle of the woods on a lake with no beach.

In town, "neighbors" lived across the driveway. At the cabin, the nearest humanity lived across the lake—two hours by rowboat or two hours walking down a winding, dirt road.

Grandma and Grandpa always took me with them golfing and bowling. Ernie's fun was hunting and trapping, and even though I would have loved to go with him, he explained to Mom and me that an eight-year-old is too little, too skittish around guns, and too noisy to effectively stalk the woods for animals.

Connection proved difficult.

It improved when we moved to a different lake where he taught me how to fish. We started simply, digging up worms in the garden and dropping a line and bobber from a rowboat. After a few successful attempts, he showed me how to cast from the shore or a dock for perch and sunfish so I could fish on my own. He had one restriction: no digging in the garden when he was gone.

This confused me. How was I going to fish without bait for a hook and line?

One thing about eight-year-olds; they are resourceful.

I thought and thought until I had a brainstorm. I put-on my swimsuit and goggles, waded waist deep into the water, and caught fish by hand. *Ernie will be proud*, I thought. That spurred me on, and I became pretty good at it.

Too good.

When he came home one night to a porch full of dead fish, he did congratulate me—after awhile—but he also decided if I was going to catch so many fish, I needed a new skill—cleaning them for supper.

Without gagging.

With all the guts and gore, the last part took repeated effort, but eventually I did it.

About two years later.

At which point I decided I was done fishing. Maybe deer hunting would be less grisly.

When I presented the idea at supper one night, Ernie laid down his fork, thought for a second, and said, "Well, you're still pretty small, but I guess you can come along."

I shifted in my chair at the counter and bubbled, "Can I get a gun?"

Mom watched Ernie carefully.

"No," he said, cautiously choosing his words. "That will have to wait until you've had safety training, but you can walk with me on drives and sit while I'm on stands."

Walking sounded okay, but sitting seemed—well, really dull. "Can I do anything else?"

"Yeah, especially if we don't get any snow."

"How?"

Ernie glanced at my mom. "Well, you don't have to make this public, but I'm color blind. I don't see red. It's brown to me. If I'm tracking a wounded deer on white snow, the blood stands out, so I'm fine. If there's no snow, the blood blends in. I can't see it. You can help me find the trail."

I looked at him sideways. "How often does that happen?"

He laughed. "A lot!"

Excited, I shifted forward in my chair. "Really?"

"Absolutely."

"What else can I do?"

"Well, you can bring your Boy Scout knife and—"

Mom's piercing eyes stopped him. "We'll see," he finished.

I didn't know what that meant, but I was thrilled. Hunting. Yes! This is what fathers and sons do in Minnesota.

The first day of season? There was no snow. I was going

to be a tracker sooner than I expected.

Ernie climbed down from his tree just as the drivers emerged from the woods. They had heard his shot.

"It was a young buck, he announced.

"Did you get him?" they asked as he landed.

He shook his head. "I hit him, but then my gun jammed. He ran right past Mike, but he only has three good legs. He went this way." Ernie took off after the tracks and broken brush, while the rest of us spread out and followed in parallel paths. The trail disappeared soon after it began.

"He's got to be around here somewhere. I know I hit him," Ernie called. "You guys see him?"

Nobody saw anything.

Maybe they're all color blind, I thought. After a difficult hour, the party stopped to regroup, spread out, then moved farther into the woods. Not really knowing what I was looking for, I kept one eye on Ernie and one on the ground ahead of me. Suddenly, I spotted something red in the yellow grass.

Nobody else was stopping. Or even slowing down. Was I seeing things just because I was so short? I decided not to say anything, instead searching the ground on my own. I found another drop, then another, the number and size growing. For absolutely no reason, I pulled off my insulated leather mitten, grabbed my knife, and continued following the blood. I heard a rustle and froze. I saw movement in the grass ahead. A brown body. White tail. Antlers.

"Found him!" I yelled. "Over here!"

The party scurried through the brush to me and the deer. While the adults surrounded the struggling animal, Ernie stood beside me and said, "He's still alive." Then, looking at the knife in my hand, he asked, "Can I use that?"

I knew what he wanted it for. I also knew it was best for the animal, but this wasn't what I had in mind when I asked to come. My eyes watered and I handed him my knife. Handle first, like he had taught me.

I couldn't watch.

After the killing and gutting were over, Ernie came and returned my knife. "I cleaned it for you. Thanks for helping. We'd never have found him without you."

"Okay," I said quietly. My stomach hurt. I was cold. I wanted to go home.

That night as we walked into the kitchen, Mom asked, "Did you guys get anything?"

Ernie recounted the experience down to the finest detail of the number of times his gun jammed. As he got to the part about borrowing my knife and dragging the animal out of the woods, I felt a strange combination of pride and guilt. I turned away.

We had our deer. I had contributed. I should have felt close to Ernie, but what they had done with my knife…

I pulled off my boots and my orange, then went into the living room, sat on the couch, staring out the picture window. His story finished, Ernie carried his gun case and orange jacket though the living room to the front hall closet. When he saw me, he extended his hand. "Thanks again."

Barely looking up, I took his hand and nodded.

"You okay?"

I looked aside and nodded again.

He stood straight, glanced at the kitchen and said quietly, "You know, if you ever wonder if something is right or not, don't do it. No matter what other people do or say. There's a reason you're questioning."

I leaned forward over my knees and examined his face. It remained calm, composed.

I thought of the dying deer and what would have happened if I hadn't found it…or if we hadn't been there in the first place. For some, hunting was a sport. For others, like Ernie, it had once been a means of survival, like when he had to feed himself and his family through the Depression and after World War II. I also knew he wanted to make me stronger. It's what fathers do.

Still, what I experienced that afternoon hurt more than I could say, more than I could admit, more than sons should feel.

"Tomorrow?" he asked.

Through the picture window, the moon's reflection rippled across the lake. I clenched my hands and nodded.

"Okay. 5:30."

By February of my freshman year at the University of Minnesota, I had also given up hunting. Father-son excursions were over. Our stepfather-stepson relationship was fine, but less than I wanted. In my vocabulary, he was still Ernie.

Then I got a momentous phone call.

"Mike, this is Ernie. Your grandfather is dying. You need to come home. We'll get you a plane ticket on North Central and pick you up."

The words stunned me. I gulped and struggled to speak. "Can I talk to Mom?"

"She can't talk right now. Everybody's falling apart up here. When you get home, you're going to have to be the strong one, okay?"

My stomach was in my throat. I mumbled something and promised to catch the plane. That night, the only person in the family operating normally—calm, rational, organized —was Ernie. Even though I resented his self-control, I followed his lead, squelching all my fear and grief.

The next day, Grandpa died, and I restrained my emotions as much as I could. I had to "be strong." My stomach groaned and ached all day.

That night, Grandma's house swarmed with family and friends, chatting and weeping, some even joking. I couldn't breathe around them. I was too sick. Clutching my gnawing stomach, I climbed the stairs to my old room and lay on the bed. I could barely breathe.

My mom knocked on the door and leaned in her head.

"Are you okay?" she asked.

"No," I complained. "My stomach feels awful."

Wiping away a tear from her cheek, she sat next to me and felt my forehead. "Well, you're not sick. Probably just nerves. A shot of brandy will fix you right up."

I pulled my arms across my stomach. "You sure?"

"It's worked for me. Want to try it?"

My muscles twinged. Just the thought of brandy hurt, but I closed my eyes, bit my lip, and nodded.

"Be right back," she said.

When she returned with a shot glass and bottle, I sat up, leaning my head against the wall.

"Drink up," she told me. "It should settle your stomach in nothing flat."

After I swigged the shot, sure enough, the brandy settled my stomach before I got to the end of the bed—settled it on the wall, on the floor, and on the covers.

I have no idea how Mom cleaned the mess so fast, how she stripped and remade the bed, where she found new clothes for me. I just remember lying alone in the dark with my arm draped over my face. I slowly became aware of the sounds in the house. Besides the commotion downstairs, there was mumbling across the hall in the other bedroom, but I didn't care. I had to lie still without moving, without thinking, without feeling. Then, I heard the door close across the hall.

A tap on mine.

I grunted.

Mom slid into the room, circled the bed and sat next to me. "You okay?"

I forced a grin. "No. Sorry about that."

"How's your stomach?"

I thought for a moment. "It's a lot better." I forced a laugh.

She grinned, then kissed my forehead, suddenly serious. "You've been hiding your feelings all day. That's not good for you. It's okay to cry, you know. You lost your grandpa. You don't have to hold it all back."

I laughed and said, "Evidently I can't anyway."

I grimaced and my shoulders trembled.

Mom gathered me into her arms, whispering, "It's okay. It's okay" as sobs wracked my body. She gently rocked me until the groaning and heaving calmed. She pulled back and wiped the tears from my face.

"I'm sorry," I said.

"Sorry for what?"

"Ernie said I had to be strong. I'm not very strong."

"Ernie," she said. "Ernie told you to be strong?"

"Yeah," I sniffed.

"Do you know where he is right now?"

I shook my head.

"He's in my old room, crying on the bed because one of his best friends in the whole world died."

"Crying? Ernie?"

She nodded at me. "You know why?"

I shook my head.

"Because even though he won't always admit it, he's strong enough to feel. That's what real men do." She stroked my cheek. "It's okay."

"Why won't he always admit it?"

She laughed. "He's German. He doesn't know he can. Give him a chance. Be strong for him, okay? Show him it's okay to cry."

Decades later, Alzheimer's Disease separated Mom and Ernie spatially, but never emotionally. She lived in a memory care unit, while he lived in an assisted living facility in the same town. Living in the same metro area, my sister Amy and I tried to ensure that Ernie could visit Mom as much as possible as the disease ravaged her mind and body. By April after a painful winter, the end was imminent.

One morning, as I drove into town to pick him up, my cell phone rang. Instinctively, I knew what it was. I pulled to the side of the road to answer.

"Mike, this is Sunrise. I hate—I mean—your—your

mother died this morning."

Tears blinded me. "Yeah, that's what I—yeah, okay," I whimpered.

"I know you were planning to see her today. Are you home or—Are you on your way? I'm not sure you should be driving."

"I'm okay. I'm in town by the railroad tracks. I'm—I'm safe."

"We haven't told Ernie yet. Do you want us to take care —"

"No! No, I'll— I'll tell him."

When I could finally breathe and see, I drove to Ernie's home, parked, and forced myself to enter. Inside the door, a nurse and the administrator met and embraced me. Mom's facility had called them. "We haven't said anything, but are you sure you're up to this?"

I massaged my lips between my teeth and nodded.

"Okay. He's in his room getting ready for you."

I took the elevator to the second floor and dragged myself down the hall toward his room. The floor nurse hugged me silently and nodded me toward Ernie's room.

The door was shut, but I could hear him organizing his stuff to go see Mom.

I stood listening as I remembered Mom's words after Grandpa's death: "He's strong enough to feel. That's what real men do….Give him a chance."

I took a deep breath, knocked, and opened the door. He was at his desk arranging last minute trinkets to bring her.

"Oh, good, Mike. You're here. I'm just about—"

"Dad—"

He jolted back and gaped at me. He knew the word was more than a name; it was a message.

I stammered. "She's—She's not— She's go—"

I couldn't even finish the thought, but my tears and straining face revealed the awful truth.

He never said a word. He just reached out for me and we cried in each other's arms. As we held each other, I remembered Mom's words so long ago: "You were always part of the deal…. He loves you."

He always had.

All the years, all the lessons, all the love gave me all the strength and interaction I needed to be a man. This day, they gave me the confidence to finally call him what I should have long ago.

Dad.

From that moment on, I always did.

After Mom's funeral, years passed, and we separated geographically. Diane and I moved first to Michigan, then Colorado. Dad moved into assisted living in another county closer to Amy. But the emotional closeness between us grew even stronger. Whenever and wherever we met, there were always new people for him to introduce me as his son. He never spoke a disclaimer or an explanation of the past. Never called me "Dora's son," "my stepson"…just "my son."

Some of his new friends never knew our story while old friends simply forgot. That's why when he died years later and mourners at his funeral gushed, "Oh. You look just like your dad," I never corrected them. He was my dad and I was proud to be be his son.

It was always part of the deal.

Butterflies and Blunders

"LOVE IS PATIENT, LOVE is kind. It does not envy, it does not boast, it is not proud. It is not rude, it is not self-seeking, it is not easily angered, it keeps no record of wrongs. Love does not delight in evil but rejoices with the truth. It always protects, always trusts, always hopes, always perseveres. Love never fails. . . And now these three remain: faith, hope and love. But the greatest of these is love."
excerpts from 1 Corinthians 13: 4-13 (NIV)

Love is one of those words you think you know…until somebody confronts you and asks, "What do you mean when you say that?"

Unlike the Greeks who have multiple words to describe the different dimensions of the emotion, the English have only one—*love*—a multi-dimensional word that eludes simple definition, especially when searching for the universal application to God, society, and fellow humans. We love our dogs. We love our shirts. We love our chocolate mousse. That's why the Apostle Paul's Love Chapter stands out so starkly against other interpretations of the emotion.

"Love is patient, love is kind."

Paul could have stopped right there. Those two clauses alone are inviting, reassuring, and positive enough to support us through our periods of rebellion and stubbornness, reminding us that God grants us second, third, and 187th chances.

They are also challenging. Humans find it difficult to be patient and kind.

Maybe not as challenging as what Paul later calls us to throw away in order to love—attitudes and behaviors like envy, boasting, pride, rudeness, ego, anger, grudges, immorality, and lies—all those human failings we cling to that stand in the way of patience and kindness.

It's almost as if he's telling us love is impossible.

He's not.

More importantly than discouraging us with obstacles and futility, Paul shifts focus to the reality of love, what makes it worth finding and pursuing, its benefits. He tells us love always protects, trusts, hopes, and perseveres. It never fails.

Even through butterflies and blunders.

"Do you want to read my book?"

Diane and I had only been dating a few weeks, so this was not the greatest ice breaker.

Why? Well, first, there was the last half hour I had spent explaining how I had spent twelve years of my life writing it plus the not-so-subtle pressure to say yes.

I could have calmly asked, "Do you like bacon?" or "What's your favorite pancake?" or better yet "Don't you just love puppies?"

But NO! I stammered and stalled, "I was just wondering…you know…if maybe perchance you might want to…I meant it's okay if you don't, but…just on the outside chance you might… Okay. Here goes….Do you want to read my book?"

I knew that was a bad move as soon as I said the words. I wanted to hide under the table.

Things had been going so well. This could mean the end.

I mean what if she gets bored and never finishes it? Worse yet, what if she hates it? What if it brings back bad memories she thought she threw into the Atlantic and she wants to rip off my ears? What if she gets a hernia hoisting my manuscript out to her car? What will she say?

I'm hopeless. I'll never talk to another woman again.

I reached into my pocket and pulled out my car keys for a quick escape.

"Sure," she said.

Her answer startled me. I sat back, stunned. "Really?"

"Yes. Do you have it here?"

"Uh…yeah." I held up my keys. "In the car. I can get it before we leave."

"Great."

Phew! I thought. *But now what?*

Now we could get back to where we should have started the night in the first place. Back to finishing the stories we had avoided weeks ago and were finally starting to reveal. Back to answering the really important questions like "Which is worse, head cheese or brussel sprouts? Hockey or parcheesi? Which is your favorite classic television character, Lassie or Mr. Ed? " (Hey! It's an important philosophical debate. Plus, how old was she really?)

On my drive home, I didn't expect her to bring up the book for weeks, and I certainly wasn't going to. Imagine my surprise when we met only days later and she announced, "I read your book."

Nothing more.

Just "I read your book."

I was petrified. What did that mean? Did she like it? Did she hate it? Did she hate ME?

"And?" I choked out.

Sensing my unease, she said, "No, I liked it."

I breathed easier, but her words missed something. Unspoken thoughts. More she wanted to let out.

"But?" I asked.

"You heard that, huh? Well…"

Here it comes. Oh, please don't hate me.

"Well what?" I asked.

"I really didn't get the beginning part. All those weird Indian names and legends and stuff? I mean it all made sense later, but it took a long time to get there."

I sighed in relief. "But the idea, the characters?"

"I really like them, especially that monster, Wayne Diego."

Wow. He doesn't show up until much later. She really read it.

And she thought about the story and ways to improve it. She went on to tell me what I needed to hear, not just what would make me feel good. Like the writing coach who had guided me through the process, she responded to the writing with honesty and truth. Without telling me it "sucked." She showed respect for my feelings as a writer, but more importantly, she maintained her integrity as a reader.

I can fix the opening, I thought. *No problem. I NEED to fix the opening.*

"That's really helpful," I told her. "If I fix it, will you read it again?"

"You'd do that?"

"Yeah. That's why I asked you to read it."

"Okay," she said, nodding.

Her smile told me we were okay, not just about the book, but also about us as a couple. From that moment, we knew this was different. Unlike we had done in relationships past, we didn't have to flatter and praise. We could trust each other, be honest with each other. We could like each other.

Maybe even more.

So I took my manuscript home and began to began to fix what I hadn't seen. For the first time, I could read what I wrote with a reader in mind.

Editing became simple. During the day, I concentrated on my opening. I tightened the prose. I explained the hazy. I exposed what needed to be revealed.

At night, Diane and I talked more and more about ourselves, our lives, our wishes, our priorities.

Finally, I finished the revision. Carefully, I reread the manuscript.

As a whole, the book was better. A more engaging story. More cohesive. Stronger.

I was grateful. Grateful for what Diane's critique had told me. Grateful she trusted me with her real reaction. Grateful for the way she relaxed when I handed her the revision and said, "Thank you."

Far more importantly than the book, however, I was grateful Diane and I were better.

I loved how we were comfortable together, how each of us was important to the other, how we let each other be ourselves, how we could always tell the other what they needed to hear.

"Do you want to read my book" was actually the perfect PHIL opening that night. From the moment the words were said, the ice was broken. Love flowed.

And still does.

Be Fine

"LOVE AND COMPASSION ARE necessities, not luxuries. Without them humanity cannot survive."
   Dalai Lama

God has a way of sending you places you need to be and introducing you to people you need to meet. Fighting Him is pointless. Even if that means talking to the homeless in an Arizona McDonald's. PHIL is everywhere.

Over the past few years as my writing habit became more entrenched, I searched for the proper setting and found myself increasingly gravitating to the nearest McDonald's.

Why? Easily available WiFi; great people-watching from squealing tykes to grizzled, grumpy curmudgeons; a constant white noise to keep me focused; and unlimited refills of caffeinated beverages.

The result? Even when Diane and I travel, finding the nearest Golden Arches becomes a necessity to maintain my routine. Being the wonderfully supportive person she is, she helps me find the closest one, the one that best meets my needs. (I like her.)

Therefore, on a recent family visit to the Phoenix area, we located the perfect store near the house where we were staying—clean, modern, easy to find, easy to drive to and from. However, it was not as perfect as I thought. God had reasons for me to be someplace else, and He wasn't subtle about moving me there.

On an extraordinarily crucial morning, the writing task excited me. I had a charged laptop. I had a topic. I had a car. Most importantly, I had time.

I left before breakfast, expecting to get a sandwich before diving into my headphones and word processing app. I drove through the sparkling sunlight and ornamental cacti, singing along with oldies on the car radio, drumming on the wheel, and smiling like a lovesick teenager. Until I found the familiar entrance. My voice broke as I pulled into the parking lot.

What was going on?

People flowed from the building like water from a gushing fire hose, their faces scowling and their heads shaking as they scrambled to their cars.

What's this about? I wondered as I pulled into the handicapped spot nearest the door. There appeared to be no emergency, no fire, no robbery in progress. Everybody was just leaving.

An *Open* sign still hung on the door. Tentatively, I exited the car as a couple emerged from the restaurant. As the husband pushed his wife's wheelchair, he explained to her, "I told you inside," he griped. "There's nothing to eat here. They don't have any meat. Let's go to Denny's."

Wait. A burger place with no meat? How does that work?

I should have heeded the man's words and followed the couple to Denny's. However, being the stubborn Norwegian that I am, I was determined to use the store's resources. I mean, they still had hash browns, soda, WiFi, and electrical outlets. That was all I really needed. I would just make the best of the unusual situation.

When I walked in, I found, despite the mass exodus, other people had the same idea I did. In the main dining room, so many pancake/potato-eating die-hards remained that the only available tables with electrical outlets were in the children's play area.

Oof. Play area. That dedicated refuge of screaming urchins unrestrained by adults or hunger, each waif blessed with a shrill, ear-piercing voice highly resistant to the most vigorous efforts of noise-cancelling headphones.

Foolishly, I decided to withstand the mayhem. It only took seconds of shuddering and twitching to realize the effort was hopeless. Drooling and muttering near obscenities, I repacked my computer and returned to my thoroughly logical wife, who rather than providing the consolation I felt I deserved, reminded me that any metro area larger than Wadena, Minnesota, had more than one McDonald's. To prove her point, she consulted her friend Google and found one equally distant from the house as the original store.

One with no play area to distract me.

"I'm there," I declared. So off I drove, and sure enough, on the same street, just in the opposite direction, there it was. Bright. Shiny.

My auxiliary office.

As I pulled into the parking lot, I realized Diane and I had driven by the building many times and I had never noticed it. As I turned off my car, although the restaurant looked okay, something kept me rooted to my seat.

Outside, the building looked larger than the Meatless Mac Heaven down the road. The other clientele entering appeared to be adult, carrying laptops just as I was. The people leaving looked like satisfied, well-fed carnivores. It should be fine. Still, my stomach gurgled and my knees twitched as I approached the door hesitantly.

Something is waiting for me. I should go home.

I walked inside and gasped. My apprehension vanished. This place was perfect!

Tables of all heights and sizes filled the room. And outlets! Throughout the space, people laughed, talked, and worked. The room breathed calm, friendly, yet businesslike.

SCORE! This is perfect. Good job, Diane!

Scanning the room for the perfect, isolated location, I

saw so many I didn't know which to pick: booths at all the windows, tables behind low walls that broke up the space, high bars hiding behind columns.

After a quick walkthrough, I chose a low table in the far corner near the front emergency exit. It had a large surface and no visible distractions nearby. I smiled and began unpacking my computer. This was wonderful.

Just as I bent over to plug in the laptop, a man tapped me on the shoulder. I recoiled, grabbing the nearest chair for protection.

"I'm sorry," he said. "I just wanted to tell you that you might have better luck with the outlets by the hightop tables."

Carefully, I examined the man. How would he know? He did not appear to be the computer type. He was disheveled with a scruffy beard and a baggy, green thermal shirt.

However, even though he seemed out of place, he also appeared to know the building well. I thanked him and explained the tall chairs usually cut off the circulation in my legs and I had a lot of work to do.

"Oh. Okay. Yeah. Okay," he stuttered as he shuffled off to a corner booth raised above the dining room like a throne. He didn't look at me. Or anybody else.

Did I insult him? I hadn't meant to, but something was off. Maybe it was his nervous delivery. Tucked into a corner that almost surrounded him, he seemed to have issues with people, yet that conclusion had to be wrong. He had tried to help an elderly, unapproachable stranger intent on other business.

I glanced over at him sipping on his soda and surveying the room, as much a part of the decor as the lighting fixtures. Relieved, I relaxed, set up my computer, plugged in, sat down... and noticed the charging monitor on the screen was blank. The outlet was dead.

My mouth twisted. I could use battery, but I never knew how long I would be writing. Especially if I got on a roll or had a moment of inspiration when the words just wouldn't stop. I preferred outlets.

I glanced at the man in the corner impassively watching the room. *I should have listened to him*, I thought

I sighed, unplugged my machine, and moved to the hightop tables, once again setting up the laptop and charger. I opened the cover and checked the monitor. Sure enough, the outlet worked. The man was correct. Before I opened my files and began work, I walked to the corner and thanked him for his help.

He smiled, extended his hand. "I'm John," he said.

"I'm Mike," I said, reaching for a handshake. A handshake he turned into a fist bump. I smiled and turned to go back to my table.

"Do you mind if I sit with you?" he asked, following me. "Do you have time?"

I wanted to say I had work to do, but his face reminded me I had been sent to this particular McDonald's for a reason. His lonely eyes told me the reason had nothing to do with writing.

At least not that day.

"Go ahead," I told him, pointing to the chair across from me.

"People complain about the outlets all all the time," he said, launching into a disjointed explanation of the building's quirks and advantages. "This one works the best, at least that's what people tell me. There aren't any in my corner, but that's the warmest place in the building and I don't really need electricity. I just need to be warm. You wouldn't think you'd need to worry about warmth in Phoenix, but it can get cold at night. After sleeping outside, you really need to find a warm place. It's not like when my family lived in Hawaii."

Nervously waving off my questions, he wouldn't tell me how he got from Hawaii to Arizona, instead comparing the Honolulu airport and Phoenix Sky Harbor. Suddenly, the conversation veered into a complaint of the noise of the jet trainers at Luke Air Force Base, but before I could comment, he gave a detailed critique of the acrobatic air teams he had seen since coming to Arizona, specifically the Navy's Blue Angels, the Air Force's Thunderbirds, Canada's Snow Birds, and his favorite foreign teams from France and Italy, although he couldn't remember or pronounce their names.

Keeping track of the conversation proved difficult, but it wasn't always his train of thought. Several times he excused himself to rearrange the chairs in the dining room, pushing them back under the tables to eliminate clutter and maintain order. Often on his way back to my table, he would direct fellow homeless to the nearest bus stop and service centers in town. When baffled customers stood in front of the combination-locked rest rooms, he was quick to their service, rattling off the four digits they needed to relieve their urinary distress.

His mind and living conditions might have been confusing, but his purpose in life was not. He was born to help other people.

An hour or so later, I told him I really needed to write. Emphatically, he apologized, gave another fist bump, and excused himself to his corner where he watched for ways he could help others in the room.

Most often, on first meeting homeless in a strange place, I am afraid and annoyed, but John was different. In the whole time we conversed, John—who had nothing—asked for nothing other than the chance to talk and serve. I felt relieved.

And guilty.

When I rose to leave two hours later, he interrupted his conversation with a homeless friend, waved, called me by name, and encouraged me to come again.

It would have been hard not to.

I was supposed to be there. I didn't realize why and how that experience had affected me until I returned a few days later.

Unlike my first visit, a mass of eager job seekers now crammed into every booth and table, replacing the spacious wide-open dining room I remembered. Oddly, it wasn't noisy. A skittish silence dominated the air as the applicants watched a distant table near the kitchen where a manager interviewed five people at a time. There would be no outlets available this day.

There weren't even any seats. Even off in his corner, my homeless friend John shared his booth with an eclectic group —a teenaged girl with a nose ring, a sharply dressed twenty-something man who kept searching for another place to sit, and a wrinkled something whose neck tattoo peeked above the collar of its Cardinals sweatshirt.

John smiled and waved at me. I waved and turned to leave.

Suddenly, a large table opened up. Before anybody by the door could move, I grabbed a seat . If somebody needed —I mean really needed—a chair, I could share, but this table was mine.

Bending over, I checked the wall next to me. There was no outlet, but I didn't care. I could use battery for a while.

God had other plans.

Just after I sat, a woman and young girl entered the building eagerly looking for a place to sit. Remembering John across the room sharing his space, I looked at the hauntingly empty chairs at my own table. I shrugged and offered the space to the mother and daughter, who grinned and gratefully accepted.

They sat, explaining that their family had just spent hours traveling from California on their way to Texas. The rest of their party was at the counter, getting food. "Is it okay if they join us?" the mother asked.

Although it wasn't what I had in mind and I didn't know how big the family was, I said, "Sure." At which point, Dad and two more daughters came around the corner with their meals. After they all sat down and arranged their food, along came Grandma.

So much for the spacious table, I thought.

But I knew this was where I was supposed to be. I folded my laptop and made room. As fellow travelers, the family and I compared notes—home states, heritage, weather, experiences—completely upending my morning plans.

Strangely, it was not an inconvenience. Not really. I learned too much about people.

While six people crammed into a van from Los Angeles to El Paso could be a disaster, this family made it work.

How?

By loving each other.

Yes, there was a hierarchy—grandmother, parents, children—but nobody was "in charge." Behavior was not forced. All smiled. All laughed. All loved being with each other. If that meant a Mexican-American family sitting with a misplaced Norske senior citizen, "Welcome to us," their smiles told him.

After they left, I looked around the room still crowded with applicants. Something was different. But I couldn't really tell what.

At first.

Then I saw John rise from his seat and go to a tense young woman mindlessly shifting her weight near the door. Leaning down, he pointed to the rest room and whispered in her ear. She smiled and thanked him. Confidently, she strode to the door and punched in the code. When the lock whirred and opened, she looked up and beamed at John. He waved and returned to his booth.

Something was different about this place. Something strange yet wonderful. I examined the customers closely.

In that room full of people, oddly enough, nobody scowled, nobody complained, nobody was there to compete. They were simply all together, sharing their space and time, sharing themselves. Sure, some were more nervous than others, but nevertheless, they were all the same, willing to offer help and willing to accept.

But there was more. What was it?

I checked the clock. I needed to get back to the house. Nevertheless, I vowed to return.

I came back two days later. My trip was almost over and

I wanted to at least accomplish some writing.

A chapter. A page. A paragraph.

Something.

When I walked in, John was back in his booth. He looked tired.

I walked to him, but before I could ask him how he was, he fist-bumped me and asked how *I* was doing. "Fine. Getting ready to return home to Parker, Colorado."

His eyes lit up. "I know Parker," he said. "My mom and I lived in Highlands Ranch."

So we sat and shared Colorado experiences until he rubbed his arms vigorously and explained he was indeed tired. "It was cold last night and we had a new guy with no blanket, so I gave him two of mine."

"What did you use?"

He waved me off. "Nothing. At least the man slept," he said.

I didn't know what to say other than "Are you going to be all right?"

He nodded and pulled out a flier for a shelter that offered showers, food, and a cot. "Yeah. I'll just go here. I'll be fine."

How? I wondered as I found a seat in the lower dining area. *How will he be fine?*

John leaned back against the wall and closed his eyes, one hand lying protectively on his bag of clothes. Then I remembered the room the last time I was there—the family, the applicants, the atmosphere.

I heard a voice, a woman—Belle was her name—say, "I've seen hundreds of these people, and every one of them— every ONE of them!— has a guardian angel watching over them. Somehow, someway, they find a way. God picks them up and gives them what they need."

The words sounded practiced, but sincere, spoken many times to many people. Words that needed to be said. As if spoken by a guardian angel herself.

"John is no different," the voice said. "John is love. John

is compassion. He'll be fine."

Even with the customers and employees scurrying about, the room became silent, a stillness that frightened me. Where was John?

Still in his booth, his head leaned back against the wall, his mouth slightly ajar. A chill sent me rushing through the tables and climbing to the corner and my friend John.

I stood, watching, shuddering. The green thermal shirt did not move. Was he breathing? I reached out and gently shook him. "John? John?"

He turned in his seat, wrapping his arms around himself. A soft snore rattled the corner.

"He's warm. He'll be fine," Belle's voice assured me.

Rising, I looked around me.

Love was in the room.

Breathing easier, I leaned close to him and whispered, "Be fine." With one last air fist bump, I smiled and left.

Michael Frickstad

Ever-Growing, Ever-Generous, and Everlasting

"DARKNESS CANNOT DRIVE OUT darkness; only light can do that. Hate cannot drive out hate; only love can do that."
Martin Luther King, Jr.

Good Friday has always been a strange event for me. For one thing, it's a holy day, but not a holiday. How does that work?

As I grew older, I reluctantly learned to accept that paradox of Western civilization, but I could not explain how to *celebrate* a day that calls the execution of Jesus Christ *good*?

I never understood that label. Yes, the resulting Easter is a joyful triumph, but how does that Friday in isolation—all its torture, suffering, gore, and death—come to be called virtuous? Why not Miserable Friday, Dark Friday, or Filthy Friday?

Still, I always recognized the events of that day as foundational to my Christian doctrine, so I took the day off from work, faithfully attended church services, thanked Jesus for His sacrifice, and prayed for His followers. However, no matter how loyally I adhered to custom and ritual, I could not understand the "goodness" of that day.

Until one revelatory church service.

Diane and I had recently changed churches and had never attended Holy Week services with our new congregation, so we didn't know what to expect. The schedule already surprised us since there was no Maundy (Holy) Thursday and because Good Friday service was scheduled in the afternoon.

Afternoon? Who in the Twin Cities goes to church in the afternoon? we wondered.

"We do," we decided. It didn't matter how few others showed up. We would be there.

As we had anticipated, when we arrived, the parking lot was virtually empty, as was the sanctuary inside. Yes, the normal thousand chairs stood carefully arranged in their usual blocked rows, but other than the twenty of us who liked to be early, no people sat in them. On stage, the praise band readied their instruments and performed their sound check.

As we made our way to our usual seats close to the front, I told Diane, "At least we have musicians. I just wish there were a bigger congregation."

"Bigger than our old church," she said, grinning.

We picked two seats near the aisle and explored the large, empty space around us. As the band practiced, other workers continued to set up the room. At the side walls, parishioners arranged long tables, covering them with dark cloth, then stacking them with loaves of bread and pitchers of juice.

I nudged Diane. "Communion?"

"Probably."

The music stopped abruptly.

Just then, another group of people, these carrying hammers and buckets of nails, entered from behind the stage and wound their way around the band members.

"What's this about?"

Diane shrugged.

Leaning against the steps that led up to the front of the stage and extending into the rows of empty chairs was a large, bare, wooden cross. The crew who had just entered placed their buckets and hammers at the four ends of the cross beams, while the band gathered in the shadows offstage to pray.

I checked the time on my phone.

"It's just about time to begin," I worriedly told Diane. "Where's—?"

She nodded, then pointed to the re-entering band. "They're back."

Almost miraculously, the musicians appeared in their places while the singers positioned their microphones. Soon, music filled the room. Even with the sparse attendance, voices and words of praise swelled, diverting our eyes from the empty chairs to concentrate instead on the cross in front of us.

Like the weekly services, after the band's three-song set, ushers passed the obligatory offering basket, which we expected. What followed, though, struck us both as odd and offensive. The usually effusive and energetic preacher delivered what appeared to be a weekday-shortened sermon.

I fumed, feeling short-changed. Here Diane had taken time off from work, we had traveled across the city, and we had arrived early in anticipation for this? That was simply wrong. I didn't want more wrong on Good Friday. What happened on that day thousands of years ago deserved more than a shortcut. Tension knotted my shoulders and cheeks.

Breaking out of sermon mode, now more as a friend, the pastor clapped his hands and told us the ushers were going to pass the baskets again. Before he could explain, I growled, prompting Diane's sharp elbow in my ribs. I didn't care. I was irate. More offering on—?

"This time, though, instead of putting in money into the basket, I want you to take something out," the pastor said.

Diane dipped her head and looked up at me. I smiled sheepishly. One thing this man was good at was surprising us, whether with his sermons or his manner. I should have expected this. *Let's do it*, I thought.

"Inside the baskets," he said, "you're going to find post-it notes and some pencils. What we'd like you to do is take them and write down the most significant sins you've ever committed, the ones that you are most grateful Jesus died for. Some of you probably need more of an encyclopedia than a post-it note, but be selective. Pick the biggest."

His smile relieved any tension in the room. Shortly after the ushers completed their rounds and the congregation had completed his assignment, the pastor moved to the cross lying on the steps and said, "I'm going to ask the band to come forward again and play during this next portion. I'll warn you, this could get noisy, but I want you to bring your sins forward and nail them to the cross. When you've finished, if you want, you can move to the side of the room and take communion before returning to your seats."

As the band played and sang, the room resounded with praise.

And pounding. Lots and lots of loud, painful pounding.

Through it all, the singing continued. Diane and I slid out of our row and got in line, following people to the cross and the frenzied hammering Strangely, by the time we got to the cross, the top, the crossbeam, and half the support beam were already covered with yellow papers.

How had that happened? There weren't that many people. Of course, the room was wider than just our row, but still…

Next to the cross, a woman handed us each a hammer and a nail. Not a tack or a brad, but a nail. A large nail. Maybe not a spike, but pretty close.

For a post-it note.

That's why there was so much noise.

Undaunted, we each took our tools and slip of paper, kneeled next to several other worshippers, and pounded our nails into the side of the main beam. It only took seconds, but the relief was profound. We stood, handed our hammers to the next in line, and headed to the side of the room for communion.

We gasped.

The room was full.

Every chair in the room was taken. Every aisle flowed with people going forward or sideways. How had that happened?

The pounding continued. Every smash crushed our breath. Every clang, every boom ached and throbbed.

Stunned, we held each other's hand and inched our way through the crowd to take communion. After the bread and juice—Christ's body and blood—we returned to our seats, our voices stronger, our praises deeper.

The hammering still crashed and rattled.

We stood singing and watching people approach the cross with their yellow slips.

And the people kept coming.

Row after row. From farther and farther back.

And through all the singing and praying, hammers nailed sins to the cross frenziedly, ceaselessly. And even through the agonizing bedlam, the rising uproar, we sang. We identified with Christ's misery and heartache, but still we sang.

Occasionally, we glanced behind us and saw more and more people coming forward. No matter how often we looked, they kept coming. Eventually, we gave up looking and simply sang.

And sang.

We suffered and prayed and sang.

Finally, the hammering ceased, the music faded, and we could breathe. The pastor stepped into the light, slowly examining the sin-covered cross. Overcome by emotion, he asked, "Have you ever seen anything so beautiful? All of that torture. All that suffering. All those sins! Think about it. All the sins ever committed!

"Then, with Jesus's unsurpassable love for each of us, He took them all. ALL! Yours. Mine. Everybody's. That's why that day is *Good* Friday. It is the day of love and sacrifice. We did not deserve it. We did not earn it. He just gave it. Because He is that good"

I caught my breath. I finally understood!

The concept wasn't new or radical. It was just true, and everything I had always overlooked was, for the first time, blatantly obvious.

We are loved.

That's what's good.

Love is the life God intended. Cleansed of anger and resentment. Connected to our fellow human beings. Joyful. Forgiven.

The miracle of that truth reduced us—Diane and me—to a hugging, laughing, puddle of tears. Through my teardrops, I spied the pastor. "I have to go tell him," I sobbed to Diane.

"Tell him what?"

I couldn't say. I just grabbed her hand and got in line behind other parishioners.

As anxious as I was to tell him how I had been moved that day, when I finally stood face to face, the words would not come. "I...I never knew..."

"Never knew what?" he asked gently.

My chin quivered and the words choked me. I pointed at the sin-covered cross. "Wh... Why *Good* Fri... Why it's good. Today, I get it."

He smiled at me, hugged me, then said, "Come back Sunday."

Well, yeah. I know. Easter.

As if he had heard my thoughts, he repeated, "Come back Sunday."

I turned to Diane who smiled at me. I looked to the pastor. There was something he wasn't saying. Something I didn't know. Something important.

"Sunday," his eyes said.

Diane squeezed my hand. I nodded.

I assumed I knew what to expect when we walked into the auditorium that Easter Sunday, and I guess I should have. However, sometimes we humans are too stubborn to recognize the obvious.

As we entered the church, I arrogantly recalled the lessons of my junior high confirmation classes: Easter is about resurrection. Jesus died and rose again.

Of course, He did. He's God. He should. I get that.

However, what that had to do with me had never been entirely clear.

Until we saw the stage.

There was the cross. The same one we had just seen on Friday lying on the steps covered in paper and nails, torn and bent, not an inch uncovered.

Today—Easter—however, it stood straight and tall on the stage—clean, no trace of paper or metal. Yes, nail holes scarred the surface, but all evidence of sin was gone.

That's why we had to come back on Sunday.

For one more lesson: The Cross—Good Friday—forgave us. Easter purified us.

And everyday is Easter.

God's love is part of the ever-growing, ever-generous, everlasting relationship He always intended for us. A relationship with Him. A relationship with each other. A relationship of peace. Of hope. Of integrity. Of love.

It's why we are here.

The relationship of PHIL.

PHIL: The Friend of Silence

IN TIMES OF CHAOS, foreseeing an ending or resolution is difficult at best. There are moments when I just want to throw up my hands and yell, "STOP," although I know the most screaming will do is give me a sore throat—and a few weird looks. Even in the toughest of times, that doesn't matter. I still want quiet.

Mother Teresa once said, "…nature grows in silence…. [the heavens] move in silence." That's the universe I want to live in. I have no time for chaos.

But it sure has time for me.

That is why discovering PHIL has been so important, especially in these months of COVID19 pandemic quarantine. No matter how tight the windows and doors, no matter the hours spent on line or streaming movies, commotion still swirls around me.

However, thanks to that late-night conversation months ago, I have learned how to conquer chaos's effects on me.

How?

By recalling the voice of PHIL—its promises of peace, messages of hope, benefits of integrity, and wonders of love —a voice following me no matter where I've gone, what I've encountered, or whom I've met.

Memory has been the key to putting this education into practice.

The night I decided to write this book, it was easy to label my inner voice as conscience, a trick of nature, or my guardian angel. However, as the project progressed, PHIL objected to all those phrases.

"You know who I am. I am not a chemical imbalance. I am not an illusion. You are not Jimmy Stewart and my name is not Clarence.

"Listen, I have been with you forever. In times of fear and struggle, my aid and counsel are always true. In times of triumph and joy, my support and laughter are always yours. See them. Claim them. Share them."

Seeing and claiming the promises and presence of God— even in the midst of turmoil—became the two-part writing process of this assignment.

First, finding guiding quotations taught me to recognize God in everyone, everything, and every situation. Besides those found at the top of each story, four special maxims uncovered the vastness of God's character.

Singer Pearl Bailey told me, "People see God every day; they just don't recognize Him."

Protestant reformer Martin Luther explained, "God writes the Gospel not in the Bible alone, but also on trees, and in the flowers and clouds and stars."

Thirteenth-century mystic Meister Eckhart declared, "Every creature is a word of God."

Poet/philosopher Ralph Waldo Emerson topped them all by saying, "The highest revelation is that God is in every man."

"…in every man."

Even in me.

The second step, claiming that revelation, was where the stories of God in the everyday came from. Each memory uncovered a new dimension in my relationship with Jesus, how He wants an inside-out relationship with me.

And everyone else.

That was His third command, what He wanted me to give others.

While God could simply shower us with blessings from above, as well as quiet the noise around us, He also wants to live inside us, helping us nurture and bless each other. He wants to speak through us and touch others' hearts. He wants to soothe us and allow His light to shine through our actions. He wants to teach us wisdom, to develop it, and to offer it.

That was the biggest goal when He told me to write this book. Throughout the process, He also explained the most effective way of accomplishing it: by seeking His peace, by embodying His hope, by developing His integrity, and by giving His love.

In other words, by finding PHIL.

Acknowledgements

SOURCES

"Dictionary.com." *Dictionary.com*, Dictionary.com, www.dictionary.com/.

"English Standard Version 2016 (ESV)." *Download the Free Bible App - Download Now or Read Online. - Android - IPhone/IPad*, www.bible.com/versions/59-esv-english-standard-version-2016.

"Famous Quotes at BrainyQuote." *BrainyQuote*, Xplore, 3 May 2020, www.brainyquote.com/.

The Holy Bible: New International Version. Zondervan Corp., 2011.

Cover art:
  Rock painting: Diane DiCarlo
  Photo: Michael Frickstad
  Editing: Roger Ballard

Editing and beta reading:
  Mary Ann Straley, Diane
  DiCarlo, Paisley Yankolovich,
  Wayne Johnson, Suzy Perry,
  Yvonne Rahm, Joel Wood,
  Jake Bland

www.ingramcontent.com/pod-product-compliance
Lightning Source LLC
Chambersburg PA
CBHW021125020426
42331CB00005B/632